YOUTH LEADERSHIP

7 KEYS TO EMPOWER YOUTH LEADERS

YOUTH LEADERSHIP

7 KEYS TO EMPOWER YOUTH LEADERS

*A Guide to Creating Exceptional Youth Programs
That Transform and Empower Youth Leaders*

DAVID A. KITCHEN

Youth Leadership: 7 Keys to Empower Youth Leaders

Copyright © 2019 by David Kitchen. All rights reserved. No part of this publication may be reproduced, distributed, or transmitted in any form or by any means, including photocopying, recording, or other electronic or mechanical methods, without the prior written permission of the publisher, except in quotations for critical review by reviewers, as permitted by copyright law. For permissions, contact the publisher, "Attention: Permissions Desk," at the address below.

MARILEE Publishing
PO Box 238, Altadena, CA 91003-0238
www.marileepublishing.com

ISBN-13: 978-1-7322482-1-2 (Paperback)
ISBN-10: 1-7322482-1-4

Library of Congress Control Number 2019905255

Chief Editor: Cynthia Gellis
Contributing Editor: Michael Lattimore
Cover Design: TDN Publications
Photos by David Kitchen, Satria Aditya & Fauxels

Printed in the U.S.A.
First Printing, 2019

Ordering Information: Special discounts are available for volume purchases by schools, corporations, associations, and others. To place an order, call (562) 548-2284 or contact publisher at the address above.

This book reflects the authors' present recollections of observations and personal experiences over time. Some names and characteristics have been changed to protect the innocent or guilty, and some dialogue and events have been compressed. Both the publisher and author(s) regret any unintentional harm resulting from the book.

First Edition

DEDICATION

To my brother, Lee Kitchen, who always demonstrated persistence in achieving his secondary education amid difficult circumstances, my sons Davidlee and Christopher for inspiring me through pursuing their dreams, and to all youth who never gave up on their dreams.

TABLE OF CONTENTS

PREFACE ix
    Challenge Facing Our Young People
    The Solution

INTRODUCTION xv
    What is Youth Leadership?
    Why Youth Leadership?
    Elements of an Effective Youth Leadership Program

7 KEYS TO EMPOWER YOUTH LEADERS
    Key 1: **E**xperiential 1
    Key 2: **M**otivational 11
    Key 3: **P**ractical (Practice with purpose) 19
    Key 4: **O**rganized 25
    Key 5: **W**atched Carefully 31
    Key 6: **E**ngaging 37
    Key 7: **R**ecognized 43

TYING IT ALL TOGETHER 47

YOUNG GLOBAL TEEN LEADERS 2019 49

DEVELOPING A YOUTH LEADERSHIP PROGRAM ... 51

TEAM ACTIVITIES THAT EMPOWER YOUTH LEADERS ... 59

SUCCESS STORIES IN YOUTH LEADERSHIP — 65
- Education-100 Years Ago vs. the 21st Century — 67
- Youth Leadership in Action! — 73
- Project Based Learning in a 21st Century School — 75
- Teaching Leadership in the Kitchen — 81
- Communication and Leadership in the Kitchen — 85
- From Youth Leadership to Billionaire Burgers — 89
- Youth Recognition in the Refineries — 93
- Discovering Engagement and Leadership Respect — 97
- Empowerment through Optimism — 101
- Youth Leadership Leads to Entrepreneurial Dreams — 105

THE TIME IS NOW TO BUILD BRIDGES — 107

APPENDIX — 111
- Program timeline sample — 112
- Budget sample — 113
- Program evaluation sample — 114
- Student feedback survey sample — 115

LIST OF YOUTH ORGANIZATIONS — 117

REFERENCE LIST — 119

FIGURES LIST — 125

ACKNOWLEDGMENTS — 127

ABOUT THE CONTRIBUTORS — 129

ABOUT THE AUTHOR — 133

*We cannot always build the future for our youth,
but we can build our youth for the future.*
— Franklin D. Roosevelt

PREFACE

Challenges Facing Our Young People
Much of the world's population is made up of children and young people, especially in poor countries. Our young people face extraordinary challenges in the world. Achieving a peaceful world demands respect for the rights of children and young people. This magnifies the desire for greater leadership.

The 2014 Nobel Peace Prize was awarded to 17-year-old Malala Yousafzai, advocating "for the struggle and the right of all children to achieve education." Yousafzai survived a Taliban assassination attempt in 2012. She had become the youngest person to receive such prize.

"This award is not just for me," Yousafzai reaffirmed. "It is for those forgotten children who want education. It is for those frightened children who want peace. It is for those voiceless children who want change."

In 2019, 15 year-old Greta Thunberg, the founder of the Youth Strike for Climate movement, was nominated for the Nobel Peace Prize. She was nominated for her activism in global climate change. Her activism began with a solo protest in Sweden that inspired student-strikes around the globe in 105 countries.

The student-strikes involved hundreds of thousands of young people. She traveled by a solar-powered boat for two weeks to speak at the United Nations Climate Action Summit. Her words to U.S lawmakers and world leaders were stunning:
"I shouldn't be up here. I should be back in school on the other side of

the ocean," said Thunberg. "People are suffering. People are dying. Entire ecosystems are collapsing. We are in the beginning of a mass extinction, and all you can talk about is money and fairy tales of eternal economic growth... Yet you all come to us young people for hope. How dare you! ... You're failing us ... The eyes of all future generations are upon you. And if you choose to fail us, I say, we will never forgive you."

Is humanity ready to accept that young people can impact these kinds of changes in the world? Young people world-wide are willing to skip class to sit in front of the United Nations building to fight against the impact of global climate change. Yet, other young people find their fight inside homeless shelters alongside parents longing for shelter and food.

Our educational institutions differ on opinions and methods for understanding the power of our youth and how to engage them and subsequently, how to empower them. How does society help more young people grow to become a vital part of social and economic change desperately needed? Perhaps, part of the challenge lies with understanding and dealing with the generational differences that have become paramount. Today, parents, schools and justice systems face a void in understanding these generational differences.

Fifteen years ago, our young Millennials, born between 1981 and 1996, were introduced to computers, social media and technological advancement never seen by their parents and grandparents. Technology made education more accessible. It also brought closer to home the fear and anxiety of terrorism, school shootings and cyber-bullying.

Millennials were born in the Generation Y era. They sport tattoos, are self-involved, untied to the value of money and always on their smart-phones. On the other side of the coin, Millennials are said to be characterized more by creativity, flexibility and a sense of social responsibility. A study by PWC, which appeared in a Forbes article, alleges that millennials will make up an estimated 50% of the workforce by 2020 (Expedite-consulting, 2019).

Now, we are in the Generation Z era, those born between 1995 and the early 2000's. This is the most wired generation. These youth grew up with technology and social media. Their exposure and access to information and world events are instantaneous. They are exposed more to and impacted more quickly by violence due to digital media. To the Boomer generation, who are considered Digital Immigrants, it is obvious these young people are Digital Natives. They are impatient with their elders who aren't as familiar with new technology.

There has become a shift to photographic experiences (good and bad) through Instagram, Snapchat and other mediums. (Hicks, 2018). Social media photos and selfies dominate our young people's world. Some of them are overly self-conscious about how people see them. They become so self-conscious about how they look they become vulnerable to others who belittle their image on social media feeds. This attacks their self-confidence, which can potentially lead to self-destructive mental behaviors like teen depression.

Exposing more young people to youth leadership can help create greater awareness of this dilemma.

Generation Zs are now in the workplace and represent nearly 25 percent of the population. Reports estimate by 2020, Generation Zs will make up one-fifth of the work force(Spataro,2019).

No matter what the generational differences may be, the numbers of issues facing our youth are growing (Social Solutions, 2019).
- Nearly 40% of children in the United States live in low-income families.
- Young people struggle with lack of employment opportunities, failures in the education system and negative stereotyping (Finamore, 2019).
- Youth suicides are rising due in part to bullying in schools and wherever youth gather in the community, classroom (29.3%), hallway or lockers (29.0%) or cafeteria (23.4%).
- 94% of youth are bullied through social media platforms and 15% online or by text messaging.
- Every year over 1.2 million students drop out of high school in the U.S. alone (Dosomething, 2019).

As a result of these and other issues, one in 10 young adults, ages 18-25, unaccompanied by a parent or guardian, experience some form of homelessness.

The Solution

Experts and leaders alike agree; youth development can prepare and equip young people to meet the challenges of adulthood. They can learn to face world challenges and to achieve their full potential. Youth development takes place through educational vehicles that procure and support strong relationships. According to a Search Institute finding in 2013, the solution lies in the five important relationship development factors: expressing care, challenging growth, providing support, sharing power and expanding possibilities (Kent, 2017).

The solution lies in our society looking at our young people through a different set of lens. It is time to look at them, communicate with them and define them as "youth leaders," not just as youth. Family, workplace and community issues surrounding our young people demand that we change the dialogue we have about our youth leaders. This book intends to develop an authentic approach to changing the depiction of young people and will refer to our youth as "youth leaders."

Why define them as "youth leaders?" Because they are influencers. They have the means to take on challenges and share their voice about community and global issues facing the world. Young people demonstrate leadership every day. They influence other young people every day through one-on-one peer pressure and through social media. They are often the leaders within their class.

The challenge to redefining them as youth leaders, however, is that young people make decisions with little regard or accountability for their actions. They are not fully mentally developed to understand how their actions impact others. Youth leadership training could help in this regard.

Redefining them as youth leaders may create a better understanding of youth challenges and better guide adults in how to best engage them. Better engagement with our youth leaders could encourage them to accept greater accountability for their actions. Greater accountability can lead to empowering youth leaders to make better choices and to do the right thing,

Empowering and developing youth leaders can prepare tomorrow's leaders today. Through effective youth empowerment, communities can do a better job of creating more services and opportunities for youth leaders. Youth Leadership training combines the impact of youth empowerment with leadership training. These two components, when merged together, create a strong foundation for fostering youth empowerment. From the standpoint of this author, youth empowerment is a viable solution that can enable youth leaders to take on challenges facing our communities and the world. The key is to implement extraordinary youth leadership programs in schools, organizations and communities around the world.

> *Generation Z . . . will soon become the fastest growing generation of employers and customers. This new generation thinks email is snail mail and Facebook is what their grandparents like. Every parent, employer, marketer and neighbor needs to understand this new generation that is poised to change everything.*
> - Jason Dorset, Leading Gen Z speaker and researcher

INTRODUCTION

What is Youth Leadership?

Youth leadership is a training concept and the practice of helping young people exercise leadership over themselves and others. It is a theory of youth development where young people learn the skills and knowledge to lead and advocate for change like education reform and even organize community activities.

Education reform, for example, has shifted how schools and educational institutions teach student learners, providing learning that is more progressive. Progressivist educational ideology, as referenced in a 2012 article on 21st century learning by Theodore Christou, concentrates on three aims:
1. focusing on the individual learner's aptitudes and interests rather than upon a rigid curriculum developed in a bygone age,
2. engaging the learner actively in the construction of knowledge, rather than merely memorizing and,
3. committing and relating to modern, current and future world concerns, not to those solely of the past (Christou, 2012).

The power of youth leadership is limitless. The framework of youth leadership development focuses on youth leader behaviors, service-leading, communication and speaking on challenges both current and future. Youth leadership training can empower young people by teaching those skills they can leverage for the rest of their lives.

Youth empowerment occurs when young people are involved in

responsible leadership activities and actively respond to the actions of creating positive social change. Empowerment, through motivation, practicality, engagement and recognition can be the bridge that enables youth leaders to cross over from passivity and helplessness about life issues to discovering solutions and taking a stand to implement solutions. Empowering young people through effective youth leadership training can transform our young people into leaders who get involved in planning and decision-making processes that affect not only themselves, but all of society.

By definition, the term youth leader has, in the past, been defined as people who work in the youth field. This definition is outdated. Our youth leaders today are the young people themselves who are capable of leading change. (Again, the perfect example is illustrated by 17- year-old Malala Yousafzai winning the 2014 Nobel Peace Prize.) When adequately empowered by the proper knowledge, resources and training, and motivated by personal experience, our young people can become the youth leaders who rise up and give voice to challenges facing our world. Furthermore, they can become facilitators, coordinators, volunteers and community activists who model leadership while partnering with adults to teach other young people leadership skills.

Youth empowerment then flourishes among these youth-adult partnerships to help both groups to teach and learn from each other. The youth leadership process becomes a 360 degree, full-spectrum process that continues to grow teams of effective leaders in our communities.

Why Youth Leadership?
Helping youth leaders master critical thinking and communications skills is a critical force to developing effective leadership. Developing confidence of self-mastery through public speaking for example helps young people to foster their communication skills and self-esteem. Helping youth leaders communicate inspires enhanced confidence in their expressions of ideas and influence. Youth leadership shows youth leaders how to collaborate with others, such as by organizing and leading group discussions in their schools, in their communities and in the world. Formal youth leadership training can speed up the process of creating responsible future leaders who take charge. Better communication skills, combined with effective leadership skills produces youth leaders capable of becoming tomorrow's leaders today. The scope of this book, therefore,

will be empowering youth leaders through the teaching of effective communication and leadership skills. Youth leadership is a dynamic force in helping young people prepare and present their ideas, mentor and listen to others and empower other youth leader. These are skills youth leaders can demonstrate in student council, group discussions, community activities and any organization focused on making this a better world.

Many youth organizations have a goal of developing the leadership potential of young people. The critical task of providing effective training programs to help our youth acquire leadership skills and knowledge can be challenging. The goal is to reach and teach others.

Current research shows that this is best accomplished through experiential and project-based learning (Bhagi, 2017). Schools provide an excellent learning environment and are equipped with an array of technology resources. Teachers have at their disposal electronic whiteboards, text books, videos, software, and a host of technology based materials to assist students with learning. What's missing is the excitement and effectiveness that experiential and project-based learning can bring about.

Specialized and focused youth leadership training enables young people to demonstrate their learned skills. Youth leadership training addresses the total spectrum of the human intelligence centers. Experiential learning engages not just the mathematical logical side, but the linguistic, creative and artistic intelligences, among others.

Low-performing academic and school drop-out issues have been a challenge for a long time. How can youth leadership possibly make a difference in those areas? Youth leadership training, through experiential and project-based learning, creates lifelong learning and long-lasting success. Research reveals two ways to create dynamic learning that 'sticks': through repetition and emotional involvement. With personal coaching and training, youth leaders can become emotionally involved in the learning experience. Infusing various innovative learning methodologies significantly increase academic success, which this book will explore. Students who succeed are those who are excited about learning and being engaged. Effective youth leadership programs provide a variety of modalities, tools and techniques to create extraordinary leaders. Engaging youth leadership programs help youth leaders discover new identities of themselves as an effective leader and competent communicator. The young people choose to continue learning because learning feels good, they enjoy it and they want more of it. In turn, they make better life decisions and are prone to lifelong success. Every parent and school should invest in this method of training, because it works.

Elements of an Effective Youth Leadership Program
There is greater need to develop extraordinary programs rather than simply good programs. Developing an extraordinary youth leadership program means creating instruction, activities and exercises that produce exceptional and positive outcomes that resonate value. If youth leaders feel the program is a positive experience and leads them to experience greater communication and leadership confidence, that is good. If, however, youth leaders use their learned skills to become model citizens and create positive change in their communities, that ideal. An effective youth leadership program must be nurtured to grow empowered youth leaders who achieve positive change in the world.

A youth leadership program works best when it is designed to reinforce positive and effective outcomes. Examining these program designs carefully, we want to be mindful not to design youth leadership programs that leave youth leaders wanting to use his or her newly acquired leadership skills to advocate negative behavior. This is the value of careful attention and nurturing. For example, what if a youth leader learned good team-building skills, then used those skills to assemble a community group advocating hatred and intolerance of others? It would be accurate to say the program taught effective leadership skills, however, the skills were not used to promote a positive outcome.

The desired goal is to develop an extraordinary youth leadership program that advocates positive and exceptional outcomes. Here is where the process of empowerment should be adequately addressed and shaped through solid adult-engagement with the youth leaders.

Youth engagement is the glue to developing the synergy with our youth leaders so they will be inspired to exhibit the right behaviors in their learning journey.

The Endowment for Health Foundation points out some of the critical benefits of youth engagement and the need to design good, effective youth leadership programs. Youth engagement has emerged as a philosophy that has become the most effective guide to help youth transition between youth and the adult stages in their lives. Interaction with model leaders is perhaps the best preparation for youth to be successful in adulthood. The Endowment study purports:

> "The youth engagement philosophy is grounded in the belief that children and youth are best served when they are active participants in their relationships and activities with adults and other youth, when their input influences decisions made about them, appropriate to their age and maturity, and when they can shape those relationships as much as they are shaped by them"(Davis, 2006).

Growing up, baby boomers were rarely engaged by adults or empowered to have a voice. In fact, they were constantly reminded that "children should be seen and not heard." One example is the story about the mom with the "boomerang shoe."

"When I tried to speak my peace as a youngster," an elementary teacher professed, "no matter where I stood, my mom would take off her shoe and throw it across the room, smacking me upside the head. All I remember seeing was my mom putting back on her shoe, as if it had boomeranged back to her."

Surely, this is merely a humorous way of describing parents during the baby-boomer age who didn't put up with impudence from their children. Youth engagement replaces this philosophy. It is now believed that children benefit by actively participating in well guided conversations about their own development.

Leaders and followers alike must use their talents and have respect for the opinions of others. We hear people exclaim "Wow! That youngster was born to be a leader." The question is though, are leaders born or made?" Some believe leaders are born into leadership positions by inheritance and destiny. Others believe training is the way for a person to achieve a leadership position. Effective youth leadership proves that every young person has the capacity to lead. An effective youth leadership program engages and challenges young people, providing many opportunities to develop and practice communication and leadership skills. These include serving as a discussion or group leader, planning an event or speaking in front of large groups and networking with organizations. Once they reach a measure of success, these young people continue to strive for more demanding, life-changing roles. They become a positive voice in their communities, a mentor to others and help develop other youth leaders.

7 Keys to Empower Youth Leaders

There are a myriad of elements to empowering young leaders. Of the many though, there are some that are universal and stand as the foundation for all experiential programs. The number one element that supersedes all others, in this author's opinion, is "empowerment." Programs that empower youth are those that create extraordinary results. In fact, the very word itself, EMPOWER, spells out the essential elements needed to design and conduct an effective youth leadership program. This book advocates that youth leadership programs must be: Experiential, Motivational, Practical, Organized, Watched carefully, Engaging and Recognition-oriented.

Institutions, churches and organizations benefit from the results of youth leadership training. The EMPOWER concept presented in this book is based on youth leadership work done by facilitators and trainers with Training Dynamics Network (TDN). Since 2005, TDN has been developing youth leadership workshops and programs aimed at transforming young people into youth leaders with extraordinary potential to impact positive change in the world.

The subsequent chapters describe these keys, make a case for why the EMPOWER framework should be the bridge to helping our youth leaders find solutions to their issues and outline tactics and methods for developing an effective youth leadership program.

In the resources and appendix section are suggested references and examples of documents that can be viewed as guidelines when creating an effective youth leadership program. Following these guidelines are stories, testimonials and interviews from leaders and entrepreneurs who have been involved with youth leadership programs. Their stories shed light on the impact youth leadership is having on our youth leaders.

Now, let's take a look at the *7 Keys to Empower Youth Leaders*.

KEY 1:

EXPERIENTIAL

> *I hear and I forget. I see and I remember.
> I do and I understand*
> - Confucious

Fire, as a means for cooking and heating, is one of nature's most essential agents of change. Its impact can be considered good and bad. Either way, fire is hot! A parent can overly beg a child not to touch fire, because it is hot. The child may be fascinated by what makes the flame yellow, orange and blue in nature. Telling the child that fire will burn when touched is important communication, especially if that child has never experienced the potential impact that fire can have. Only when the child experiences getting near its radiant heat or touching the fire will he or she actually understand that mom and dad are right - fire IS hot!

Using fire as an example may be a bit extreme, but it conveys clearly the point that human beings unequivocally learn from their experiences, good or bad. We learn and grow from the events we experience in our lives. This effect is even more enhanced with our young people.

Training youth leaders to feel empowered begins by introducing them to activities that engage them through experiential learning. Experiential learning has been proven to be the most effective method of creating and sustaining engagement.

Teaching young people skills through an experiential method can, and usually does, make an undisputable impact on their behavior. Experiential learning reinforced learned behavior. Studies on learning styles conducted by International Psychiatrist William Glasser and other researchers found that human beings remember more through experience. Glasser asserted these interesting facts on how we learn:
We remember:
- 10% of what we read
- 20% of what we hear
- 30% of what we see
- 50% of what we both see and hear
- 70% of what is discussed with others
- 80% of what we experience personally

The foundation for creating experiential learning begins with understanding the five basic senses we use as human beings; sight, hearing, smell, taste and touch. Each sense sends information to the brain that helps us perceive the world around us. Consider an example of how understanding this process can help engage young people in a learning environment. Picture this classroom scenario:

> A trainer has given two youth groups an exercise to complete and has instructed each group that when finished they may take a break and enjoy snacks and refreshments. The youth groups of six begin their assignments and collaborate on assembling an art puzzle project. The project is designed to teach them teamwork and creativity. Each participant is handling one or more pieces of the puzzle **(touch)**, while at the same time listening closely to the instructions given by their leader **(hearing)**. The participants, while working as a team and working against time, begin to **(smell)** warm chocolate cookies being delivered for their break. Some youth are smiling, anticipating the tasty treats. Each youth is looking **(sight)** carefully at the other puzzle pieces to see how his or her individual pieces match up. When both groups finish assembling the puzzle, the youth congratulate themselves with hugs and high-fives **(touch)** and when instructed, retreat to the back of the room and enjoy **(taste)** the delectable treats of

cookies, brownies and milk. The youth are smiling, laughing and expressing to each other how they cannot wait to work on the next project.

This is merely a simple example of how the five senses drive and enhance experiential learning. Experiential learning is heightened in an environment that promotes a variety of learning methods; visual (sight) kinesthetic (touching), auditory (hearing) and holistic (feelings).

Experiential learning has been proven to be one of the most effective aids in teaching young people and is a hands-on approach to learning new skills. This learning style has also been referred to as project-based learning. The big picture here is that experiential learning occurs through participation and actions. Project-based learning, employed by many progressive institutions in classroom activities, is a component of experiential learning. Experiential learning sustains results that enable youth to find the answers and/or resolve a problem. This is a shift from lessons that are *teacher-focused* to those that are *real-world focused*. Combining these strategies creates an extraordinary youth leadership experience. .

> *While content of any learning experience is important, the particular content is irrelevant. What really matters is how students react to it, shape it and/or apply it.*
> - Rob Riordan, President of High Tech High School

The success of a youth leadership program, depends on the youth leader's ability to experience what it feels like to use a skill. Also important is what it feels like to express thoughts and interests clearly and logically to others. It is vital to develop experiential learning through a series of participant-oriented activities that inspire young people to demonstrate a skill. Often, it takes a participant sharing their experience to drive home a particular lesson learned. Take this scenario for example:

In a Los Angeles middle school, the classroom was filled above its normal capacity. Grabbing the attention of 40+ students added to the difficulty for this teacher. The teacher, Ms. Galinda, introduced herself to the class, shared her background, the class' objectives for the year, and invited each student to do the same. Observing the sign-in roster, it appeared that only half of the students signed in. The middle school students appeared bored. Some, if not most, were disengaged, not only with hearing Ms. Galinda's background but with hearing other youth introduce themselves.

One student named Rafael, wearing tattered, faded jeans with holes, black Vans shoes and a faded, red, plaid shirt, shared his background. He shared that his upbringing was in gang-infested neighborhoods and he was grateful to not be in jail. He shared that until last year, he was defiant of rules and didn't think about the ramifications of his perceived association with those who affiliated with gangs. "One time," he explained, "I was accused of skipping school one day and getting involved in a liquor-store heist. The store owner claimed he identified me through a school yearbook picture that the police showed him." He said he was apprehended by the police and interrogated. With a stream of tears rolling down one side of his face, he said he told the detectives he was at school on that day, and that he could not have been involved. "The detectives did not believe me," he said. Finally, he explained, after checking with his school the police discovered he had indeed signed the classroom roster for each and every class on that day. It turned out that one of his past teachers had developed an activity rewarding students who had 100% school attendance. He explained he had reluctantly volunteered to sign up, telling his classmates, "Signing all the class rosters that day was evidence that I was in school on that day of the robbery, and therefore, could not have been at that store." For that reason, he shared, he signs in for class each and every day and has a better appreciation for rules. "Those class rosters kept me from going to jail and saved my life."

The following day in class, remarkably, the teacher had no further challenges getting her students to sign the class-room rosters. The emotional experience shared by this student was remarkably educational and inspired them to new heights of class participation.

The only source of knowledge is through experience.
- Albert Einstein

Conducting activities that are based on experiential learning and promote order, structure and respect for others creates a strong foundation for nurturing youth leaders. Create scenarios or role plays that help them feel what it's like to stand up straight when speaking, and to show active listening techniques. (nodding head, smiling when understanding, etc).

Consider these questions when designing youth learning activities: How can we encourage a young person to be prepared for a lesson? What activities can make young people feel enthusiastic about contributing to a group discussion? What motivates youth participants to communicate with others and pay attention?

Experiential learning engages the potential capabilities of our youth leaders from every angle of their young minds. This learning style fully engages what some psychology professionals describe as activating the four quadrants of a person's whole brain. In some academia circles, this is referred to as whole brain teaching.

Whole Brain Teaching
The Whole Brain Teaching concept is one that behavioral experts find sets the stage and maximizes engagement tied to experiential and project-based learning. Experiential learning, with the understanding of whole brain teaching, focuses on the way the brain is designed to learn. Chris Biffle, a former college instructor, started the Whole Brain Teaching movement back in 1999. The whole brain teaching theory offers an approach for understanding brain functions through the four quadrant model: logical, organized, interpersonal, and imaginative. Instead of looking at people as "right brain" or "left brain" learners,

Biffle's theory claims there are four brain quadrants that respond independently of each other. These four quadrants respond to teaching styles in different ways. Biffle designed a learning styles inventory designed to help learners discover their preferences for dealing with facts or feelings, for using logic or imagination, and thinking things through, by themselves or with other people and in an organized fashion.

Whole brain teaching strategies emphasize active learning, which is an experiential learning technique. Trainers may play soothing music during instruction, or encourage youth participants to draw or act out what they are learning. Ever notice some people are visual learners? Some are better taking written tests. Others are better at working with their hands.

Movement supports the brain function that supports remembering, emotions, language and learning. In primary education children are directed not to move in class. Teachers ignore the fact that movement is crucial for the brain function that supports remembering, emotions, language and learning. Most teachers are not aware of the kinesthetic learners in their classrooms.

Participants in youth leadership programs, who play together, fail together and actively learn together, will remember more. This is an environment where learning and doing is imaginative, inspirational and experiential. Workshop facilitators and youth leadership coordinator's use the principle concept: *They See. They Touch. They Learn. They Do.*

Youth participants SEE what needs to be done and how to do it. They TOUCH the material needed to execute the activity. They LEARN how to complete the task assigned to them. They DO by being allowed to think for themselves and create a solution.

Experiential participation engages youth and helps them form the habits that activate the conscious part of learning, which then trains the subconscious to remember the action taken.
Creating a judgment free environment promotes trust and engagement. Learning takes place when the youth leaders experience either a success or failure. Experiments and failing moments are sometimes viewed differently between youth and adults. For example, young people

riding bikes and wrecking them is play time, along with sharing these experiences among friends.

For adults, the danger of their children wrecking the bikes and the cost of repairing them are frightening and not looked upon as a laughing matter. Adults tend to focus on the dangers instead of the opportunity they have given their son or daughter to learn a skill, establish independence and have some fun.

Kids are not afraid to fall down or break things. Kids go all out to see how things work. Failure is one of their greatest learning lessons. Their lack of fear creates the perfect conditions for them to experience different things and to stretch their imaginations. Therefore, it is a good idea to assign them activities that push them to go beyond their limits. Don't worry. They'll survive. And they will thrive from the lessons learned.

> *Many of life's failures are people who did not realize how close they were to success when they gave up.*
> - Thomas Edison

There is power in failure and no better way to learn than those moments learning to ride a bike. Some people may remember the difficulty in learning balance and falling off when they first learned to ride a bike. Some experiences may have been traumatic just from the fear of falling. This may conjure up wild and uncontrolled thoughts about Dad not putting the bike together well. Images may have haunted them of riding a bike; wobbling side to side, feet falling off the pedals and tumbling over the front handlebars with the bike landing on top of them.

Okay, that may be a bit of an exaggeration. But this may explained why adults tend to focus on the dangers rather than the learning opportunity. The point is this: whether or not the experience was good or bad, we learned from it. Consider this unique learning perspective illustrated from a story told by Marshall Ramsey, cartoonist and speaker:

Late one Monday afternoon, a lone man sat on a park bench, looking down with his face buried into his hands. At a time when he should have been at work, he wasn't. He had recently been laid off from his job. And now, depression had wrapped around him like a strait jacket. About 25 yards away was a little boy with his mom. The boy was trying to learn to ride a bike without training wheels and so far, as best as James could tell, was failing miserably. But the kid kept after it. Instead of moping about it, the kid just got back up, dusted himself off and tried again. Until finally, about an hour after James first noticed him, James put his bag down and walked over to the boy and his mom. "I've been watching you, young man. Good job!"

The mom smiled and said, "Thank you." The little boy adjusted his bike helmet and said, "Thanks." The boy said something in a different voice to James: "I didn't quit. I didn't lie there in the grass feeling sorry for myself. I got back up and dusted myself off. I could've not gotten back on the bike. But I would've missed a lifetime of thrills. I didn't quit. You shouldn't either." James was taken back by the kids' comment. He wondered, "How did he know?" The little boy looked just like James did as a small child. That made James start to think. Kids have no fear of failure. They try things. They experiment. And then James realized an undeniable truth: Failure isn't falling off the bike. Failure is not getting back on.

James Washington fist bumped the little boy and said thank you again to his mother. He then walked back toward his house and prepared to "get back on the bike" (Ramsey, 2012).

Experiential learning is a predominant key to creating an effective youth leadership program. It is learning that stimulates the brain. Incorporating the "feeling and experience" of activities that model responsible behavior makes experiential learning a key component to empowering youth leaders. Today, young people are actively sharing their experiences through digital platforms. One of the best illustrations of this is through the use of social media. Social media, just by its usage, has become a tool for experiential learning.

Social Media - Experiential Learning in the 21st Century
Seven-out of-ten Americans use social media to connect with one another, engage with news content, share information and entertain themselves (Pew Research, 2019).

Some 30 years ago most employees knew little to nothing about their leader outside of work. In the 2000's, it became more acceptable to know leaders on a personal level. Today, it's the norm to know them on a personal level and be connected with on social media. Through social media teacher and student end-users are tracking their learning, taking pictures of the progression of student projects, posting homework, and writing about the significance of a document or a posted photo.

According to the social media site INC, leaders should use social media to; share their experience or expertise with others, connect with people on a human level across geographies, time zones and demographics, and stay connected to colleagues and industry developments to maintain relevance in their respective fields.

Today, experiential learning involves end-user training to teach youth leaders responsibility in using social media, and to advocate "user accountability" with other youth leaders. The theories and application of experiential learning enables youth leaders to learn powerful lessons from their interactions with the world and integrate new learning modes, like social media.

Experiential learning driven by technology leads to powerful and effective academic learning, which harnesses the power of phenomenal youth leadership training. Learning leadership experientially is the same as learning to fly a fly a kite.

Experiential Lesson on Leadership: Flying Your Kite Right!
Leaders can learn a lot from the process of flying a kite. Flying a kite is truly an experiential learning process. As kids we spent every chance we could to fly our kites. We'd race home after school, take off our school uniform, throw on t-shirts, jeans and tennis shoes, scramble for the kite and spools of string and race to meet our friends on the rooftop of the three story project building.

Just the anticipation of tying the string and attaching the kite tail gave us an adrenaline rush. Rows of mom's old leg-stockings tied together made the best kite tails, to keep the kite from going into a tailspin. Then we would hold the kite up and let the wind take it, releasing and pulling the string just enough to keep it balanced. Our spools were huge, with four or five 500-yard spools of string all tied together, up to a mile in length. Every day we challenged ourselves to see how far we could let the kite fly. Sometimes, we would lose a kite and would have to buy a new one the next day. Most days, we would fly our kites so far that we couldn't even see them. Only the tautness of the string indicated whether the kite was still attached.

There are many correlations between the experience of flying a kite and leadership principles:

- Bigger kites need more wind. In leadership, larger projects need more team effort.
- You need lots of string to fly a kite long distances. In leadership, the longer the project, the more resources needed.
- Strong wind resistance is needed to fly a kite. In leadership, strong differences of opinion can help a leader achieve higher goals.
- A good weighted tail helps keep the kite balanced. In leadership, a strong line up of talent helps ensure the team maintains balance.
- Knowing when to pull and release the string is crucial. In leadership, leaders must use various leadership styles, knowing when to push and when to release.
- Sometimes you can't see the kite but can feel the resistance on the string. In leadership, you can't always see what the team is doing but leaders need to hold tight to measures that monitor progress. Resistance serves as a guide to improvement.

KEY 2:

MOTIVATIONAL

Why fit in, when you were born to stand out!
- Dr. Seuss

Every youth leadership program benefits from participants, trainers and stakeholders who are motivated to make a difference. Therefore, it is incumbent upon the developers of youth leadership programs to ensure the activities and subject matter taught are motivational. Motivation promotes participation and collaboration. Motivation is the force that encourages youth participants to get to know each other and work with other team members.

Motivating youth leaders to collaborate, share and present their ideas is a key to the effectiveness of a youth leadership program. For example, in some learning environments young people are hesitant to open up to collaborate or participate. Adults and young people alike typically behave with resistance during the early phase in a new training or learning environment. Perhaps they feel inhibited by directives where active participation is expected and required. With young people, some of this relates to feeling nervous, or simply not trusting the process of sharing with others. Employing a fun ice breaker activity usually helps eliminate some of the anxiety that prevents them from collaborating and sharing with others. Having fun during a learning process motivates participants to trust and open up. Creating the right activity is the motivational key to developing an environment that is anxiety-free. Young people thrive in environments that get them to abandon their fears and explore new learning ideas. The goal is to find a method that motivates youth leaders to get acquainted, try something new and have some fun doing it.

Collaborating and Sharing Ideas

Motivating our youth leaders to collaborate and share ideas gets them involved in their classrooms or meeting discussions. Participation is the preferred method for solving problems, arriving at decisions or making plans, rather than them being directed. Motivating youth leaders to participate sets the stage for good discussions that are open, purposeful and help youth leaders reach win-win solutions. When youth participants are motivated, discussions take place in a respectful and team centric manner. Every youth leader participates and contributes.

Sometimes participation may get out of hand. Some participants will be more eager to share their ideas than others, or even have a tendency to take over conversations. In this case, a motivational technique, or "dangling the carrot" approach may need to be implemented. Setting ground rules or agreement statements in collaboration with participants at the beginning of a youth leadership session helps establish a learning environment that promotes mutual respect. For example, establishing an agreement that no one gets a snack break until everyone has shared can possibly motivate youth participants to help manage themselves to ensure others participate. They become motivated by the anticipated snack time that lurks just ahead.

Incorporating the right motivational tools can help maintain focus on achieving desired outcomes. The goal is to get young people excited about being transformed into empowered youth leaders. Youth leaders are motivated by recognition. Youth leaders can also be motivated by being offered a role as a class leader, whereby they can have a say in how the class is run. By creating the right motivation, youth leaders can be inspired to make positive changes at their schools, in their communities and in the world. In certain environments, motivation can occur from the circumstances that young people encounter every day. Young people living in poor third-world nations might be more motivated to speak out on the need for clean water. Youth leaders who walk past homeless shelters daily may be motivated to create a youth movement to eliminate homelessness in their city, state or nation. These are just a couple of examples where circumstances can create the motivation for action.

There are many theories describing the models of constructing motivation. One in particular is referred to by behavioral experts as the *ABC of Motivation*. There are two relevant studies about transforming young people into youth leaders. One recent study on the ABC of Motivation is referred to it as the *Self Determination Theory*. This model describes the core motivations as Autonomy, Belonging and Competence. These are considered the new ABCs. This model asserts that young people are more likely to be enthusiastic and motivated when they feel they have some measure of control over their environment and are recognized for their competencies.

Another model provides an even more relevant construct for creating a learning environment that motivates youth leaders to modify their behavior. The Lagacee Group *ABC of Motivation* theory describes motivation from a performance stand point. Lagacee refers to it as understanding the mental engine components that drive motivation performance. This model breaks down motivations between Antecedants (response/prompts), Behaviors (desired or undesired) and Consequences (reinforcement) (Murray, 2019).

The antecedents are the conditions that are pre-existing and creates stimulus to perform a learned behavior. For example, a young person who is often bullied may avoid contact with others. A young person who cries out for peer acceptance, or craves attention may engage in behavior to gain a reaction from other people. Effective motivation practices, if crafted well, can replace such behavior through understanding what prompts such behavior. Modeling a more accountable behavior, exploring feedback, rewards and goals may achieve more responsible and empowered behavior.

Some facilitators rely on using consequences to drive a desired behavior. This can be through negative or positive reinforcement, punishment or avoidance. While consequences may drive behavior more than reward, in practice it tends to demotivate people and stifle participation. In summary, youth leaders require the motivational reinforcement to fully participate in the empowerment process.

Pushing participants into doing something extraordinary can show them they are capable of accomplishing a remarkable task, if they put their minds to it.

Let's take a look at what a good push will do. This story has been told in many variations by many authors, but makes the point well:

> A very wealthy man invited some of his closest associates in to see it. Towering over some 1500 acres of mountains and rivers and a spectacular scenery, out back was this gigantic swimming pool filled with alligators. The wealthy owner explained "I value courage more than anything else. In fact, I think that courage is such a powerful virtue that if anybody is courageous enough to jump in that pool, swim through those alligators and make it to the other side, I'll give him anything he wants, anything – my house, my land, my money."
>
> Of course, everybody laughed at the absurd challenge. Suddenly there was a splash and to everyone's amazement they saw a guy swimming for his life across the pool. After several death defying seconds, the man made it to the end of the pool and quickly leaped out unharmed. The billionaire host was absolutely amazed by the young man's courage. Sticking by his promise he offered the man anything he wanted - his house, his land, his money – "Anything whatsoever", said the host.
>
> Breathing heavily, the swimmer looked up at his host and said, "I just want to know one thing – who pushed me into that pool?"

In other words, what prompts the kind of extraordinary behavior we want to see or reinforce? This ABC model sheds better light on to how to motivate youth leaders in a learning environment to embrace empowerment and do what needs to be done. This model asserts that behavior can be motivated by feedback and consequences.

Using the Lagacce model, developers of youth leadership programs can determine what types of activities should be created to transform our ordinary young people into extraordinary youth leaders. To get more technical, there a few common behaviors youth participants typically demonstrate and different motivations for each. Understanding and creating a structure that addresses each of these would provide a solid foundation for making a youth program that motivates youth leaders:

1) **Social Attention** - Young people who behave a particular way to get some form of attention or a reaction from other people. For example, a child might engage in a behavior to get people to look at them, laugh or play with them. A good way to motivate these participants would be to grant them a leadership role that puts them front and center.

2) **Activities** - Some young people behave in a negative way to be chosen for a group or activity based on their own preference. For example, a young person may not like a group or team they were assigned to. They may simply have a need to have say in the decision. A good motivation for these participants may be to give them options, and allow them to voice their likes and dislikes. Incentivize them to act responsibly to achieve the desired result.

3) **Escape or Avoidance** - Some young people want to avoid any and all participation whatsoever. For example, youth participants might engage in aggressive behavior so that they are not chosen for an activity. They may come up with excuses for not attending the workshops consistently. A good motivation in this situation may be to encourage them, in the beginning, to observe more than participate. Connect them with more supportive youth and slowly acclimate them into the streams of activities (Saggers, 2004).

An engaging youth leadership program that motivates young leaders is a program that empowers them with the option to choose their activities. Providing options motivate youth leaders to come to life and leap into action. This technique encourages youth leaders to start a conversation about getting involved and taking action (TeachThought, 2017).

Motivation can be intrinsic or extrinsic. Intrinsic motivation derives from an internal or personal satisfaction of accomplishment. Extrinsic motivation, on the other hand, usually comes from another person, or from an outside source, obligation, or reward. Motivation, both intrinsic and extrinsic, is a key factor in the success of students at all stages of their lives, especially in their home, school and community environments.

Developing an engaging youth leadership program can encompass an assortment of motivation styles: giving students a sense of control, creating a threat-free environment, using positive competitions, encouraging collaboration, giving participants responsibilities and recognition and making things fun.

The behavior of the youth leadership facilitator plays a key role in promoting the proper motivation also. Youth trainers should make an extra effort to allow participants to work together, encourage self-reflection, show enthusiasm themselves and know their students. As the old saying goes, "People don't care what you know, until they know that you care." This is particularly important for youth leadership program facilitators.

> *People often say motivation doesn't last. Neither does bathing. That's why we recommend it daily.*
> - Zig Ziglar

It's important for facilitators to implement the right motivational tools. The ingredients include having fun, making time for nourishing snacks and creating a safe place for learning. Trainers, youth leaders and parents play a huge role in the success of an engaging youth leadership program. Having the right trainers is by far one of the most valuable contributions to engaging youth leaders. Some facilitators and trainers present training in an energetic way that inspires youth participants to enjoy learning leadership, even learning leadership outside of a traditional leadership workshop environment. In fact, the food industry has now gained the interest of young people wanting to learn culinary arts.

Anyone who enjoys cooking, and is captivated by the sheer joy of people or teams competing, surely are big fans of the Food Network shows. Some culinary schools and professionals are developing culinary programs designed to teach leadership skills and motivate would-be youth chefs to perhaps launch a career in culinary arts.

Learning Youth Leadership in the Kitchen
These days the Food Network television channel has proven that cooking in the kitchen is not just for adults anymore. There are at least seven TV network shows, like *The Greatest British Baking Show, Kids Baking Championships* and *Chopped Junior* (kids version of *Chopped*), that promote the educational, competitive and inspirational talents of kids putting their fryers to test.

The question is, "Can teaching youth leaders culinary skills motivate them to learn communication and leadership?" Sure it can. It is being done every day.

Chef Sam Paano, a youth trainer and owner of *Gourmet Conspiracy*, asserts, "It's vital to learn to communicate effectively in the kitchen. Working in a kitchen environment requires both leadership and communication. Prep chefs must continually let each other know what order is coming up, how long before each dish needs to go out and any changes to the orders."

One of the unique institutions teaching youth leadership and communications skills in the kitchen is the Detroit Food Academy (DFA) in Michigan. DFA not only introduces youth to the food business, but it's showing youth that leadership is a key ingredient in the culinary field. The kitchen is their classroom.

Working with local educators, chefs, and business owners, DFA, is helping young people, ages 10 to 24, to build leadership, business, and entrepreneurial skills. "It uses food because of how tangible it is, and how many different issues, ideas, and histories [it] touches," says Jen Rusciano, DFA co-founder and executive director (Warfield, 2019).

DFA teaches leaders from both an academic and a business perspective. On the academic side young people are taught communication and leadership. On the business end they are taught budgeting—from planning a food item they want to sell, to pricing the ingredients and setting a cost with the goal of making a profit. From its leadership and fellowship programs, some students, through DFA's business side, receive a stipend to work for one of two product lines; Mitten Bites and Slow Jams that features products designed and crafted by DFA students.

In a 2019 *Yes Magazine* article, Rusciano explained that because home economics classes have been phased out of most U.S. high schools, many young people no longer have hands-on experience or the same opportunities to apply math skills in the kitchen. She says what DFA is doing goes beyond teaching kids about healthy food and healthy cooking. It motivates them and shows them "how to think about entrepreneurship, equity and production in the food industry, and getting a wide range of experiences to help them understand food sovereignty"(Detroit Food Academy, 2019).

Success stories by Chef Sam Paano and Jen Rusciano start on page 81.

KEY 3:

PRACTICAL
(Practice with Purpose)

> *You earn your trophies at practice.*
> *You pick them up at competitions.*
> - Anonymous

A high school senior, Johnny, sits with his parents over dinner discussing his plans for transportation to school. Looking at his parents with a big smile on his face, Johnny comes up with what he thinks is a great idea.

"How about I use your car dad to drive to school?," says Johnny. A little amused, Dad responds, "Son, you barely started practicing how to drive and you don't even have a driver's permit yet. That just wouldn't be practical."

Exploring an effective solution to a challenge requires some form of practicality. Same applies to developing an effective youth leadership program. The practical goal for creating an effective youth program is to provide youth development training that fosters youth-adult partnerships and to empower youth leaders become engaged, skilled and model youth leadership skills for others.

Practical, by definition, refers to the actual doing or use of something. It differs from teaching theory or ideas. A youth coordinator with ten years of experience would have practical knowledge of how to work with young people, as opposed to someone new to the field who only knows theory.

A practical youth leadership program would be one developed with lots of room for leadership practice and with purpose. Again, the purpose for incorporating activities that are experiential and motivational is that it inspires youth leaders to step into their ability to lead change.

The best way for a youth leader to grow leadership skills is through the facilitation of practical application that allows them to practice these skills over and over again. For example, a method for teaching communication skills is to have youth participants repeatedly give speeches, realizing that repetition creates learning.

Practice is necessary to ensure that lessons are remembered and can be duplicated to achieve the desired end result. . Engaging youth leaders with a practical program allows them to process and share their experience. In this case, *practice makes permanent* and they can now apply their learned experiences to real-life situations outside the classroom, in an effective demonstration of what they've learned.

The professional martial-artist and Hong Kong-American actor Bruce Lee shared a profound expression on the art of practice:

> *I fear not the man who has practiced 10,000 kicks once,*
> *but I fear the man who has practiced one kick 10,000 times.*

The benefits of youth leadership programs that are experiential, motivational, and practical can be tremendous and global. These programs can serve as the practical foundation for empowering youth leaders all around the world to generate positive social change.

Youth leaders today are the voices being heard on social media advocating for education reform, clean water, homelessness and green space initiatives. An effective youth leadership program strengthens personal and social development in these youth leaders, empowering them to become the voices of change for generations to come.

Here is a short inspirational story from Indian mythology to emphasize the benefit of practice in achieving a goal:

> Once, Lord Indra got upset with Farmers, announcing there will be no rain for 12 years, leaving farmers unable to produce crops. Farmers begged for clemency from Lord Indra, who declared rain will be possible only if Lord Shiva plays his Damru (drum.) When the farmers reached Lord Shiva, he repeated the same thing, agreeing to only play the Damru after 12 years. Disappointed, the farmers decided to wait until 12 years passed. But one farmer regularly continued to dig, treat and put manure in the soil and sow the seeds, even with no crop emerging. Other farmers were making fun of him. After three years all the farmers asked the ridiculed farmer "Why are you wasting your time and energy when you know that rain will not come before 12 years." The one farmer replied, "I know that the crop won't come out but I'm doing it as a matter of practice. After 12 years I may forget the process of growing crops and working in the field, so I must keep doing so that I'm fit to produce the crop the moment there is rain after 12 years."
>
> Hearing his argument Goddess Parvati praised his version before Lord Shiva and said "You may also lose the practice of playing the Damru after 12 years." The innocent Lord Shiva, in his anxiety tried to play the Damru, if he still could. Hearing the sound of Damru, immediately there was rain. The farmer who was regularly working in the field had his crop emerged immediately, while the others were disappointed (Total Dreamer, 2017).

The Lesson - Practice is what will turn your dream into reality. Practice doesn't always make you perfect. But, it keeps you prepared. The more you practice, the more confident and skillful you will be when the opportunity arises.

Allowing youth leaders to practice making their own decisions increases their decision making abilities. It allows them to have a voice, a say so in matters that concern them. This is highly practical. It enhances their level of accountability and leadership skills. Therefore, one of the important keys is to develop a practical youth leadership program that incorporates a youth development curriculum that intentionally builds social, behavioral and educational skills.

Surveys over the years show that young people who have practiced leadership activities in youth leadership programs outshine their counterparts in creativity, commitment, confidence and discipline. They become youth leaders who attend post-secondary schools and colleges with solid organizational skills and the confident ability to lead change.

> *A student feels motivated to practice,*
> *if he leaves his lessons feeling capable.*
> - Frances Clark

Training experts are not the only ones advocating the importance of practice. UK based musician, writer, and podcaster, Andy Mort shared an interesting take on this subject. Mort is founder of The-Haven.com, a membership community dedicated to support and encourage 'gentle rebels' to find and share their voices. Here is an excerpt from one of his blog postings where he talks about reminding himself of the value of practicing with purpose:

> **If You Don't Know Your Limits, You'll Never Reach Your Full Potential -** Practice time is your opportunity to take things to the limits of your current ability. It is your time and it must be regular. We can often make the mistake of believing we don't need to practice. Nothing is more dangerous to a person than believing those who say they are 'gifted' or 'special', and allowing those kinds of labels to do the work for them. Just study cases of child superstars/prodigies and you get an idea of how damaging it can be to adopt the belief that you are extraordinary, whether there is truth in it or not.

Practice and Rehearsal are Not the Same - There is a big difference between these two concepts and it is worth reflecting on. Practice is essentially the verb of deepening and sharpening your skill set – it's putting in repetitive processes in the attempt to break new ground. It is private and perpetual. Rehearsal on the other hand is preparation for something specific. As a musician it is the time and effort put into getting ready for a show. It has a very definitive public endpoint that you are working towards.

Andy purports a person doesn't need others to understand the practice. In fact if it IS neat and pretty you need to make some changes. Practice should be hard, gritty, and full of failed attempts at hitting the target. This is the essence of why practicality is important to empowering our youth leader.

KEY 4:

ORGANIZED

> *One of the core organizing principles of my life is that success comes through a delicate balance between making things happen and letting things happen.*
> - Robin S. Sharm

Transforming young people into empowered youth leaders require organized communication. Effective leadership programs teach youth leaders to communicate in an organized manner. This means communication structured with a captivating opening, a compelling message supported by facts and closing statement with a strong call to action. For example, a student council president must organize and clearly communicate a series of speeches to council members in a manner that compels fellow members to understand at the heart level and take appropriate action.

The same principle applies to organizing an, effective youth leadership program or workshop. An organized workshop will contain a clearly defined opening, a middle and a closing. Like a good speech, the opening engages and hooks the participants, the middle is a bridge through the program and the closing is a call to action and celebration of accomplishments.

The most effective learning environments hit the sweet spot between structured learning and the chaos of having fun. Organization keeps a program focused and moving forward. One of the more effective ways to create that type of environment is to organize the program based on peer-to-peer relations, ages, etc (Lovestrand, 2011). More on this is spelled out below. Here are some ideas for organizing and structuring activities. These can help get young people to open up, participate and focus their energies on learning valuable skill-sets capable of transforming them into global leaders.

Set Ground Rules
Establish and agree to adhere to ground rules for expected behavior. This is most effective when these are established during the initial meeting and agreed upon by the entire group. Keep these posted in visible location during all subsequent meetings.

Utilize Club Officer Roles
Nominating and electing youth leaders to leadership roles as officers of a youth leadership session organization provides experience in formal leadership roles. Additionally, serving as officers increases their self-confidence and further invests them in the experience.

Establish a Meeting Agenda
Consider setting a time limit for the business portion of the meeting or on individual discussion topics to keep meetings from running over time.

Make it Fun to Break the Ice
Include icebreakers (introductions) and team building activities to incorporate elements of fun and familiarize youth with each other. If adults are participating in the meeting, encourage them to participate in the activities as well. This equalizes participants and establishes shared respect for both parties. The Michigan State University 4-H club has a great online resource with activities and examples of opening icebreakers (Martin, 2018).

Involve Youth in Planning
Meet with youth officers or teen leaders in advance of the meeting to prepare. Always involve youth leaders in the agenda writing process and resist the temptation to simply hand an agenda over to youth. Experience in the process assures they understand the topics to be discussed and are invested in the discussions to follow.

Use a Fair System for Decision Making
This is often in the form of parliamentary procedure or Roberts Rules of Order, but a group can also choose to use consensus-building strategies. Make sure all group members' voices are heard.

Celebrate Successes
Appropriate recognition reinforces successes and provides appreciation for youth leaders running the projects, meetings, etc (Reich, 2005).

An effective organization technique that can help facilitators and trainers coordinate and monitor youth participant is by forming discussion groups based on age or competencies. Some facilitators call this technique *peer grouping*. Peer grouping assures that participants are more likely to feel comfortable participating.

In fact, a study by the United Nations Children's Fund, cited in the United Nations World Youth Report, found that at times, peer educators were more effective than adults in establishing norms and changing attitudes. However, that is not always the case. There is one exception to this rule, and a benefit to matching slightly older youth participants with those who are younger. In after school programs it was shown that having slightly older students helping younger students helped bond students to the program long-term (Lovestrand, 2011).

Additional elements might include, involving them in planning activities and crafting an agenda to stay on track, just to name a few, sets the foundation for a well organized program.

Evaluating the Need and Building the Program
In organizing an effective youth leadership program, additional key steps include; evaluating the need of both the youth leaders and the sponsoring organization, the funding of the program and the support needed.

Take extra care to determine the volunteers, standards and training personnel needed to launch the program. For example, youth leaders who have gone through a leadership program make excellent volunteers and/or trainers. Their experience can shed light on how to engage the youth leaders based on their own experiences in the program.

Then, establish tools, resources and parameters to evaluate the effectiveness of the program. Consistently review and modify the program to ensure that all the elements of what is needed is available: clear objectives, ample materials, adequate background knowledge and training instruction by the facilitator. Make sure there is time built in for student practice and clear understanding of the activities. Of all things, ensure that proper recognition, acknowledgements and assessments are clearly built into the program.

> *The key to a learning environment is structure.*
> *- Cara Caroll.*

Design and organize the program in a way that is uniquely specific to the youth leaders who plan to attend. With this said, build a program or workshop with the following in mind:

- Have a specific purpose or end goal in mind.
- Be mindful of dates, seasons and times that may take youth away from attending regularly.
- Be specific about the goals the workshop or program is set out to achieve.
- Determine the size of the group and the scope of the program (Katemba, 2015).

When building a youth leadership program, include developing a budget that ensures all the cost for venue, material, activities, staffing and miscellaneous expenditures are comfortably met.

After which, it is beneficial to take into account the strategy and takeaways the sponsoring organization requires. Above all, beware of deadlines, deadlines, deadlines. In helping fellow volunteers map out their action plans, one leadership colleague, Jonathan Eckman, shares with his team:

> *Deadlines are closer than they appear.*

It is very befitting. Think of it as the side view mirror concept.

KEY 4: ORGANIZED

Programs That Shine Have Social Media in Mind
Organize and develop youth leadership programs that teach youth leaders to use social media responsibly and to help them become accountable digital leaders in their schools, families and communities. Help them make sound decisions through critical thinking concepts and use social media to identify community needs, develop life skills and engage in the process of making this a better world (Self Help, 2019).

> *A life lived in the service of others is worth living.*
> - Albert Einstein

Organizing a youth leadership program that includes social media elements helps youth leaders share knowledge and experience with others faster. Social media is one of the most powerful learning tools because social media platforms make sharing information instantaneous.

In the 21st century information and knowledge comes fast in the form of an Instagram post, a tweet, a blog post, or a video on LinkedIn or YouTube. Experts and successful business owners attest to the power of social media and its influence, as noted in a *Today Online* article:

CEO Tan Wee Keng, Tollyjoy Baby Products – "There is no ignoring the influence of social media in consumer habits, personal opinion, and as we have recently witnessed, the outcome of electoral decisions. Important as it is as eyes and ears to the market, social media alone does not dictate leadership direction."

Founder Malvin Foo, The Maven Co. – "Borderless, instantaneous and engaging – it is hardly breaking news that social media has become ubiquitous in our daily lives as viral videos and articles from Facebook and Twitter take over as conversation starters."

It's estimated about 45 percent of Fortune 500 CEOs are engaged in social media.

An effective youth leadership program is one that is organized with purpose, meets the needs of the youth leaders and the sponsoring organization, and is adequately-funded and engages youth leader with relevancy and structure. This will help youth leaders explore making the impossible possible.

KEY 5:

WATCHED CAREFULLY

But the watchful care of the parent is endless. The youth is never free from the danger of grating interference.
- William Godwin

It is important to understand that even a well-developed youth leadership program, along with its activities and training methods, must be watched carefully. This can be understood as *monitored and evaluated*. To maintain a motivating, practical and experiential learning environment, the program must be developed with strategies that enable facilitators to watch program activities carefully. Facilitators need to know the youth participants will participate in activities safely.

Organizations supporting or funding a youth leadership program want to know that measures are in place to ensure the program's safety and success. And of course, parents of youth leaders want to be reassured about safety and trust it will be worth the cost, in time and money, for their child to attend.

Young people need to feel safe and supported. A safe environment promotes active uninhibited participation and willingness on the part of youth leaders to "let go" and perform. Trust is the key.

To summarize, youth leadership programs are watched carefully by two means: Monitoring and Evaluating. To ensure the program will be effective, build monitoring and evaluation process before starting the program. Define a clear purpose for the program and its activities. Monitoring and evaluating helps to outline expected results and identifies which elements of the program are producing the desired results. During the program stakeholders funders and facilitators may need to make adjustments. Sometimes unexpected results require a change in strategy. The benefits of program participation may not be evident immediately while monitoring progress. That's why a post program evaluation can address some of the challenging aspects of measuring outcome

Organizations wishing to develop a well monitored and properly evaluated youth leadership program can take a few cues from the Stars Behavioral Health Group in Long Beach, California. In 2010, Stars Behavioral Health Group, produced a report on the effects of implementing large-scale training programs. The report included an analysis of developing plans and strategies to ensure evident-based practice fidelity, monitoring quality assurance, and measuring outcomes. As a result of the report, Dr. Hewitt B. Clark developed the Transition to Independence Process (TIP) model aimed at improving the outcomes for young people.

Among other developments, the TIP model offers seven specific guidelines that helps to focus program activities on youth and young adults making the transition to adulthood. These guidelines are:

1. Engage young people through relationship development, focusing on their future,
2. Tailor services and supports to be accessible, coordinated, appealing, non-stigmatizing, and developmentally appropriate.
3. Acknowledge and develop personal choice and social responsibility with young people.
4. Ensure a safety-net of support by involving a young person's parents, family members, and other informal and formal key players.
5. Enhance young people's competencies to assist them in achieving greater self-sufficiency and confidence.
6. Maintain an outcome focus in the TIP system at the person, program, and community levels.
7. Involve young people, parents, and other community partners in the TIP system at the practice, program, and community levels.

KEY 5: WATCHED CAREFULLY

Dr. Hewitt noted, for the purpose of his study, that the first guideline focuses on engagement with a young person through relationship building. That relationship establishes the primacy of the young person's future and well-being. The second, third, fifth, and seventh guidelines focus on the positive inclusion of a young person's choices at a personal, program, and community level. His study goes on to express that every child looks forward to the day when he/she is no longer controlled by the decisions of adults. He points out that parents, as well as young people worry and face anxieties about reaching that point. He believes these feelings are part of youth and family development.

When monitoring activities to determine how successful a team-building activity is, it is necessary to be extra watchful. This is because some activities, like trust-building for example, require careful oversight to ensure no one gets hurt, physically or emotionally. Monitoring is extremely important as facilitators are often encouraging participants to "take-risks," to let go of their inhibitions and to "play full out" in trust-building activities.

These trust-building activities are conducted to demonstrate the importance trust plays in establishing teamwork and collaboration. We're not talking about having participants climb trees and hold each other upside down by the ankles to demonstrate the benefit of trust. We are talking about ensuring that participants are able to be physically or emotionally vulnerable, free of either physical or emotional harm. For example, a physical trust-activity may involve a participant being blind-folded and trusting another participant to lead him or her safely from one destination to another. An emotional trust-building activity may be one where two youth participants share with each other a secret about themselves as effort to practice listening or disclosure skills.

Facilitators must ensure trust-building activities are conducted in a safe manner. When done right, these activities help youth leaders to break through the fear and anxiety that prevent them from embracing their leadership potential.

The key is to give youth participants the feeling of being in control, when in fact training facilitators are maintaining control and monitoring at all times. These are moments in a training environment when youth leaders will fully let go, participate with no fear or anxiety and maximize their learning potential.

While facilitators monitor the activities of the program, developers of youth leadership programs evaluate the effectiveness of programs from a big picture perspective. Developers want to ensure programs accomplish the goals envisioned for the program. Some behavior experts assert that monitoring and evaluating youth-focused programs can be challenging for many reasons, such as:

- Adolescence is a time of growth and change, so the level of participation to be expected may not be evident,
- Young people are highly mobile so it may be difficult to keep track of participants for follow-up,
- The benefits of program participation may not be evident immediately, and thus harder for most programs to measure (Empower, 2016).

While this may be the case in some instances, it further proves why an effective youth programs must be monitored and from the start, and through-out the program' duration. The value of post-program evaluation allows the measure and outcome of the program to be concluded properly.

Even ten years ago, small organizations partnered to create programs that changed the way youth programs reinforced learning. Programs developed by providers like Training Dynamics Network provide experiential learning in communications and leadership. Career Dreams, Inc. reinforces the idea that all youth are brilliant. Inspired Learning Organization teaches techniques to create a positive, safe space by setting ground rules and success agreements that motivate youth leaders to be successful.

Evaluating youth programs ensure effectiveness, enable program organizers to make necessary changes are made and creates a platform with repeatable learning strategies.

Ongoing monitoring and evaluation of an evidence-based program is essential because these processes provide information to the staff implementing the program as well as the community stakeholders. Using measurable data on a continual basis helps program coordinators to:

- evaluate the effectiveness of team activities,
- understand whether the program has been implemented with a reasonable level of fidelity,
- identify areas for improvement, training, or adaptation;
- justify to stakeholders and funders that the program is effective; and
- determine whether organizers want to expand, cut, or abandon the program altogether (Youthgov, 2007).

Evaluating a Program

There are two steps to evaluating an evident-based program. One way is through process evaluations, which measures what the program proposed to achieve. The other is through outcome evaluations, which measures what outcomes were achieved. Let's look at both:

>**Process Evaluations** - Knowing the process of an evidence-based program is important. It helps to understand how the program activities are connected to the outcomes achieved. Process evaluations can also help identify the level of implementation and areas needed for additional training, resources, or support.

>**Outcome Evaluations** - Outcome evaluations allow a youth program developer to understand what happened as a result of implementing the evidence-based program. They can reveal whether the program achieved the desired results

Factors that may influence how to evaluate the program include: cost, availability/flexibility, knowledge of program, operations and outcomes, trainer skills and expertise and youth leader and stakeholders feedback.

These evaluations will ensure that measures are in place to assure the programs safety, success and repeatability.

KEY 6:

ENGAGING

> *We rise by lifting others.*
> - Robert Ingersoli

Youth engagement has emerged over the past three decades as a philosophy that guides the interactions of young people with the adults in their lives in empowering ways that best prepares them for success. Before youth empowerment can occur, engagement must take place. Youth empowerment is a process through which young people are encouraged to take charge of their lives. They do this by learning methods to address their situations and then taking action.

This empowerment allows youth leaders to transform their consciousness through their beliefs, values, and attitudes. It begins, however, with active engagement, which sometimes conflicts with traditional classroom control methods. Engagement among youth leaders themselves sometimes takes on a different look from the organized learning environments we tend think of. Sometimes engagement is, in an unorthodox way, fueled by what facilitators describe organized chaos. Consider this scenario:

> A K-8 public school substitute teacher in Minneapolis, Idiana walked into her colleague's class to observe student behavior. She expected this school to be a little tougher than other places she had taught.

Yet this was no run-down inner-city school. Instead it was a new style brick-and-glass building with bright natural lighting, and students looking sharp in their dark-bottom/white-top uniforms. The students weren't shy and seemed inquisitive. She had been warned about students being "a little wild." The teacher in-charge was conducting an activity that seemed unorthodox for a traditional public inner-city school. In this class of predominantly Latino and African-American students, he said something loudly to get their attention. Half of the students looked up. The other half started chatting out of control. Soon, most were on their feet, dancing to some type of rhythm. The substitute teacher gazed on as the class seemed to love this particular activity. But she felt the activity appeared to be chaotic, with the students flat out goofing off!

She smiled at the futility of it all, as if this rumble of chaos was probably the norm for them. Then suddenly, she noticed it all came to a halt with just a few simple hand-claps. The teacher clapped twice, summoning the students to take their seats. The students stopped and clapped twice. The teacher clapped three times, followed by the students clapping three times. Each student subsequently sat back in their seats. The teacher then asked for volunteers to share with the class the activity he or she chose to demonstrate, and how that activity relates to the real world. Indeed, the observer was amazed to witness what first appeared to be students running amuck, quickly transformed into a model student environment with students sharing their experiences. How could this be?

The Power of Organized Chaos

Organized chaos is defined as a complex situation or process that appears chaotic while having enough order to achieve progress or agoal. A fine example of organized chaos may be the game of football, which is described as, "organized chaos and a nightmare to keep under control." The colliding of helmets and shoulder pads as players scramble to gain yards or even inches can be viewed as chaotic. Yet it's held together by some form of organized engagement. The same structure can apply to working with youth leaders.

Young people essentially find their way to success. Have you ever seen a classroom cluttered with students laughing out loud, perhaps even tossing things back and forth between each other? Sure, no teacher or trainer wants a chaotic scene like that. Think about it though! In a classroom environment like this youth participants would be in their most uninhibited moment of trust and participation as they experience unadulterated engagement.

Engaging participation by having fun makes a program memorable and keeps youth craving more. Young people (as well as adult learners), love to get out from behind their desks, move around and have some fun while learning.

Designing activities immersed with fun and learning at the same time can create the kind of learning that traditional control-teaching can't match. In some circles it is referred to as *edutainment,* education disguised as entertainment. Bear in mind, however, no matter how much fun they are having or seem to be behaving out of control, they must be reminded of the end goal in mind.

This type of loose structure fosters an engaged environment in which youth leaders can thrive. It is an environment where youth leaders are more present and responsive to each other. This format sparks collaboration and stimulates the feeling that anything is possible. It fosters critical thinking, causing them to think for themselves. What a concept! Above all, it generates enthusiastic ENGAGEMENT.

The concept of *organized chaos* harnesses the power of heightened learning and independent thinking. What an exciting environment to be part of - one that is fun, playful and full of energy. The classroom may look like it is out of control, when in fact it isn't.

Once engagement is stimulated, it is then best to assign lessons and learning activities in team settings. This can help calm the "chaos" so that the youth are now focused on the lesson plan in a smaller team setting. Don't forget to make the lessons interactive. Remember, the goal is to train our youth leaders to make independent choices. It is a huge win-win when the youth participants are not taking themselves too seriously (Shaw, 2019).

> *People learn best in moments of fun.*
> \- Ralph Smedley

The youth engagement philosophy is grounded in a practical sense of *vision and possibilities*. It is grounded in the belief that young people are best served when they are creating healthy relationships and engaged in activities. This philosophy further asserts that youth participants shine when their input influences decisions made about them and when they can shape those relationships as much as they are shaped by them (Davis, 2016).

When youth acquire the authority and ability to envision, map, execute, critique and challenge their reality, it opens them up to opportunities to change the world. Give our youth leaders tools to collaborate, problem solve, brainstorm and reflect on their experiences. And then, allow them to unleash what they have learned out into the world. Youth leadership facilitators, coordinators and trainers find great results from helping program participants see the correlation between "imaginative" and "real-world" applications of life. It empowers youth to examine their own behavior and how their behavior impact themselves and others. Consider these suggested steps to create youth engagement:

1) Provide youth leaders with the information and resources necessary for analyzing issues that affect their lives. Help them develop strong strategic thinking skills in order to enable them to act as change agents in their communities.

2) Encourage them to use their passions for good. Guiding youth to use their passions and creativity to share positive messages or bring attention to issues they care about will allow them to find purpose and harness the power of their actions in creating change.

KEY 6: ENGAGING

3) Guide them to believe that their voice matters without judging or criticizing their ideas. Empowered youth understand that their voice makes a huge difference in this world and that all ideas are worth exploring. This will give them more motivation and fuel to continue strengthening their own power for change.

4) Help them to understand that people will not always want to listen. Help youth to understand that not everyone is going to respond positively. Some people may not be ready to hear what they want to share. It's important to let youth know that when someone doesn't listen to them, not to take it personally.

5) Lead them to learn that sometimes even the most fabulous idea may need a bit of practicality. Guide youth leaders to understand that implementing visions and ideas take time and must be realistic and well thought out.

6) Help them to know that there are different stages to a project. While the first stage is having an idea, there are many stages after that. This will help them understand the full process and not get stuck on the first stage of an idea.

7) Help young people develop habits that they can sustain with internal guidance, rather than external 'suggestions' or prodding. Good habits produce sustainable leaders. Youth who have good habits for their own well-being and personal growth become strong leaders on their own.

8) Give youth leaders a chance to learn from their failure. Let them know that failing is not a bad thing, it's actually an important learning opportunity. By finding out what went wrong they can improve and make it better the next time. Often the way to success is through failure.

9) Employ success stories to counteract negative messages about young people. Encourage youth leaders to speak about their triumphs often, and to share their victories to reinforce the positive change that has occurred. This will inspire more positive action and a broader foundation to support their work.

10) Invite the youth leaders to launch a project. Support them to implement their project once they feel they have come up with a good strategy. Allowing them to carry out their vision with encouragement and support will be an engaging experience. Make them feel supported in their process (Gladstone, 2013).

These engagement strategies can transform the beliefs, values and attitudes of youth leaders. It can inspire them to take charge of their lives, and prepare them for success in the world at-large.

> *Young people should be at the forefront of global change and innovation. Empowered, they can be key agents for development and peace. If, however, they are left alone on society's margins, all of us will be impoverished. Let us ensure that all young people have every opportunity to participate fully in the lives of their societies. A society that cuts off from its youth severs its lifeline* -- Kofi Annan (Doonething, 2019).

KEY 7:

RECOGNIZED

> *What gets measured gets done.*
> *What gets recognized gets done even better.*
> \- Robert Crawford

Nothing tears down a human being faster than not being recognized for a heart-felt effort. This is particularly true with young people. Recognition not only boosts participation in engagement, but can be the foundation for increased productivity and better performance. Young people participating in a youth leadership training environment thrive on the opportunity to see their names on a Top 10 list, or to receive a certificate or trophy for coming in first, second or third in a fun competition. Recognition gets them excited. They feel good about being rewarded. They long to repeat the activity to continue that feeling of excitement when recognized.

Adult and youth leaders alike benefit from recognition. A youth leader might grasp onto an opportunity to help others if he or she anticipates being recognized for doing so. Some may view this as just a servant leadership mindset that requires no recognition. Chances are greater that youth leaders will eagerly step up to serve when they feel important and appreciated for helping someone or accomplishing a goal.

Some proponents may believe that recognition must be monetary or something tangible. Would an employee continue going above and beyond their job duties if there were no additional monetary gain? Consider this scenario:

> Sam is an engineer for a small tech company. His company pays him top dollar for his ability to draft schematics and design alarm systems for big companies. His company has been downsizing and hasn't offered raises or bonus payments for two years. At the annual company meeting, Sam was recognized for his work on improving the existing alarm systems and infrastructure for the company. Sam was excited about the award. His remarks, when accepting the recognition, may have come as a surprise to some of his fellow colleagues. In spite of not receiving higher monetary compensation for his efforts, he expressed to his co-workers, "I enjoy the work I do and I look forward to continue making more improvements to make our working conditions safer and better."

In the real world, the above scenario represents more of an exception than the rule. But the feeling expressed adequately applies in learning environments where, instead of money, recognition is the reward in a classroom setting and where a teacher will give positive recognition to top performing students. It gives the students a sense of appreciation. Others will take notice, which encourages other students to want the same recogniton.

A person who feels appreciated will often do more than what's expected. It is important that any youth program includes some sort of recognition for the participants in order to be effective. This can happen during a final session or at a special ceremony as long as everyone who was involved in hosting the program is present, recognized and rewarded for their efforts.

Youth programs conducted by organizations like Training Dynamics Network, the 4-H Youth Development Program and Toastmasters International hold special ceremonies for their youth leaders. Some of these feature a showcase event, where participants have the opportunity to demonstrate their newly acquired skills for each other, family, friends and other stakeholders. Following the presentation, each participant is given a certificate for completing the programs.

Recognition helps youth leaders feel good about what they have accomplished and strengthens their self-esteem. It gives them a sense of closure and satisfaction for completing projects and activities. Making young people feel good about accomplishing something motivates them to strive for future successes.

Recognition promotes positive behavior and invites others to want to be part of the fun. Just the same, it is also important to recognize anyone else who has played a role in the youth leader's success in the program.

Even in the business world leaders who show recognition and sincere appreciation to their teams gain a significant return on their small investment. (Community Tool Box, 2019).

> *The power of recognition is one of the strongest forces for stimulating human and social action*
> - Lowell Milken

When incorporating recognition into a youth leadership program, be sure to recognize everyone involved, not only the program participants. That would include:

Volunteers - These are the heart and soul who help the program reach its goal. Whatever their contribution, include them, as they are considered an integral part of the organization.

Stakeholders - Involving your stakeholder helps to increase morale and cohesiveness. Recognizing the funding that made the youth leadership program possible is a polite gesture. Supportive officials and community members are excellent outreach connections, especially if they were instrumental in this accomplishment.

There are a variety of methods for recognition. Additionally, there are numerous benefits:

Methods of Recognizing
- special events or activities as part of an ongoing program (before the program ends),
- contests, skillathons or designed challenges,
- scholarships/sponsorships to colleges or education institute
- hand-written thank-you notes,
- newspaper, website acknowledgments and social media posts,
- opportunities to present as a model presenters for training workshop,
- showcasing youth in marketing materials and PSAs
- Retreats or field trips,

Benefits of Recognizing
- Sets up participants for authentic leadership opportunities.
- Creates individual learning portfolios showing achievements.
- Creates lasting mementos of the experience.
- Encourages participants to give back and help others get rewarded.

Once the decision is made on the purpose, the style of the recognition (publicly or privately) and its affordability, an organization should have a pretty good idea of what form a recognition celebration might actually take. As the old saying goes, "a little recognition goes a long way." Recognition transcends more than just the formality of giving out awards. It creates a warm and fuzzy feeling and lasting memories.

TYING IT ALL TOGETHER

Advocating for more youth leadership programs increases the opportunity to transform more of our young people into youth leaders. Arming them with the right tools and resources truly empowers them to use their voices, serve their communities and make positive impacts in our world. The seven keys tie together all of the elements needed for the EMPOWER concept to work:

- Training youth leaders to feel empowered by introducing them to activities that engage them through *experiential* learning.
- Maximizing youth leader opportunities to collaborate through *motivational* techniques to encourage youth leaders to share and present their ideas.
- Ensuring that the program is *practical* helps youth leaders attain realistic goals, with the purpose of fostering stellar communication and leadership skills.
- *Organizing* the program and activities using agendas and creating objectives is a vital key to keeping youth leaders focused and moving forward, while still making room for autonomy and fun.
- Understanding that even a well-run and organized youth leadership program must be *watched carefully.* Monitoring and evaluating the program throughout helps determine measures are in place to ensure the programs' success.
- Developing individual and team activities that are actively *engaging*, in order to spark collaboration and foster an environment where youth leaders are participating, committed and accountable.

- Ensuring youth leaders are ***recognized*** and feel good about completing projects, which strengthens their self-esteem about what they have accomplished.

These are the EMPOWER keys to building bridges for our youth leaders to cross over from just being seen and not heard to being outspoken model citizens who become our future leaders. Understanding the core elements of creating effective youth leadership programs opens the door to helping families, schools and communities to empower our youth leaders.

We're doing a disservice to young people if we give them only information and technical skills. We must prepare them to fulfill their role as citizens, and to LEAD.

-David Tarver, President, Urban Entreprenuership Initiative, Inc.

YOUNG GLOBAL TEEN LEADERS

Developing effective youth leadership programs can assist in building strong bridges to mobilize phenomenal youth leaders to advocate for positive change throughout the world. Organizations that foster social change in the world promote ways to recognize these types of youth leaders.

For the eleventh year, the We Are Family Foundation (WAFF) proudly announced its yearly Three Dot Dash Global Teen Leaders (GTLs), representing 15 countries on six continents. This award features 19 year-old teens who are innovating technology and harnessing creativity in the areas of clean water initiatives, cancer research, civic engagement, urban forestry industries, machine learning or tackling modern day global challenges. This proves that youth leaders can create change on a global level.

The following page shows pictures of these youth leaders. Information on each of these young people changing the world in 2019 can be found at the website: www.threedotdash.org/2019-global-teen-leaders.

YOUTH LEADERSHIP: 7 KEYS

2019 GLOBAL TEEN LEADERS

PRESS RELEASE   AT A GLANCE

Alana Daly Mulligan

Amonge Sinxoto

Anna Ferti

Archika Dogra

Ari Sokolov

Audrey Pe

Brian Kamule Kamenju

Chiara Amisola

Danish Mahmood

Diana Vicezar

Faith Florez

Hasham Tanveer

Hunter Williams

James Wellemeyer

Kesava Krupa Dinakaran

Lucas Scherpel

Mahika Halepete

Malcolm Asher

Marissa Sumathipala

Melissa Khasbagan

Peyton Klein

Priya Mittal

Priyanka Shrestha

Rocio del Mar Aviles-Merc...

Sarah Chadwick

Shreya Nallapati

Tanishq Kumar

Teevysh Yuva Raju

Veenadhari Kollipara

Viraj Mehta

DEVELOPING A YOUTH LEADERSHIP PROGRAM

The entire world benefits from organizations, schools, churches, for-profits and not-for-profits, who actively and strategically participate in sponsoring or conducting youth leadership programs. The *7 Keys to Empower Youth Leaders* is based on the belief that effective youth leadership programs can be the bridge to EMPOWER young people to become strong youth leaders.

While there are varied approaches to and purposes for developing a program, there are some elements that are fundamental to any program's success. The following guidelines are recommendations for creating effective programs that actively engage youth participants. See Appendix for example of planning timeline for a youth program

These guidelines are the culmination of extensive research, testing, practices, professional opinions and implementation. They have been proven to serve as an effective core for youth leadership programs that have purpose and engage youth leaders.

Invest in Key Steps to Implement a Youth Leadership Program
There are a plethora of ideas, methodologies and development approaches for creating youth leadership programs that engage youth leaders. Organizations really just need to ask just one question: "What is absolutely essential to create an engaging youth program? "Here are some general steps that organizations or program developers should

take into consideration when developing a youth leadership program that empower youth leaders:

- Evaluate the audience and objectives for the type training.
- Determine the participant's group, purpose and identify key players (i.e., trainers, coordinators, etc).
- Create a realistic budget for program resources.
- Determine strategies, create an action-plan and define the program take-aways.
- Determine standards and training methods.
- Build the program with youth leaders and stakeholders in mind (program funders, sponsoring organization).
- Plan for post-program evaluation.

Knowing the Audience
The first questions to answer when developing and planning a leadership training program is *What audience is the program intended to reach?* Then drill a little deeper. Will the program be for all youth ages or only for older teens? The ideal outcome for an effective program is determined by the make-up of the class. The program will be more engaging if the participants share a similar age range and have similar experiences. Discuss this factor with the school or organization for which the program is being created.

Know Where Youth Are Developmentally
In public speaking, it's important to know the audience. This is a must. The same applies to developing a youth leadership program. The ages between 10 – 21 years old are a critical time of development. This is the time when young people are establishing their sense of personal identity. They are developing the ability to see things from another's point of view and a commitment to a system of values. They are learning to be goal-directed and principle-oriented, rather than parent-directed and peer-oriented.

In modern society, family ties are growing weaker. Peer relationships are becoming more important. Many lack experience, however, in dealing with this new inter-dependence. It is recommended to be aware of age sub-groups when planning. For example, an eleven year old may not possess the capacity to understand or demonstrate the learning capabilities of say an 18 year-old. Therefore, keeping age ranges grouped closely together in a program generally makes the lessons more applicable to a specific age group. Grouping together ages 10 - 13, 14 - 17 and 18 - 21 will keep the learning in these groups more relatable. There are exceptions to this rule, as noted in the following story:

> In one Los Angeles Catholic school, the principal asked if a 14 year-old could register, attend and participate in a program being developed for 16-18 year-olds. At first glance it appeared that the values and learning capability of the 14 year old kid would be too far below those of the older teens. The fear was that the 14 year would not be able to keep up with the learning concepts. At the discretion of the youth facilitator, the school and the parents of the 14 year old, this kid joined the class.
>
> It turned out that the 14 old student demonstrated cognitive abilities beyond his years. In fact, his comprehension and communication skill-set exceeded some of the 18 year old participants. The result? The older teenagers began to feel a bit intimidated, causing them to step up their game, becoming more responsible and focused in their team activities. After all, no one wants to be outshined by someone four years younger. In this exceptional instance, having a broader age-range of students enhanced the learning experience.

Determine the Program Objectives

Writing measurable program objectives is the first important task. Will the program focus on teaching life-skills to at-risk students? Or, will the objective of the program be to teach class leadership skills to potential student council participants? Incorporate a system to gauge if the objectives can be reasonable achieved.

Essential Areas of an Engaging Youth Program

Build a youth leadership program with young people in mind. They need to feel comfortable participating in scheduled activities and voicing their opinions. The following are seven components that complement the seven keys to empowering youth leaders. This can be used as a guide.

One effective system is the SMART theory. (Specific, Measurable, Attainable, Realistic and Timely). After creating an objective, ask the questions: Are the program objectives specific? Can they be measured by staff? Can the expected behavior be achievable and realistic? What are the expected time frames for completion of each activity? For the program itself? Here are some sample objective statements:

- Each youth participant will learn two goal–setting techniques by the end of the training session.
- 90 percent of the youth participants will be able to list and demonstrate three active listening techniques by the end of training.
- Each youth participant will be able to present a 10 minute speech organized with an opening, fact-based examples and summary conclusions.

Determine the Leadership Topic
After creating the objectives, decide what topics will be featured in each session. Topics can include; communication skills, creativity, leadership development, teamwork, problem-solving and respect for others. Students who engage in problem-solving activities learn transferable skills they can apply in their everyday lives.

One of the first activities should be one where youth participants of the group can get to know one another. These are known as ice-breaker sessions and will help set the pace for the rest of the training program. Not only do young people need to learn how to be effective leaders, but also they need to know how to be good followers. This includes learning how to build good leader–follower relationships and learning how to build strong team attitudes.

Help Build Leadership Identity
Each young person develops a sense of his or her unique identity. This helps to define the levels of training needed for the youth participants. Their identity can be reinforced through interaction with other people. Young people need to know that they have special talents that are unique to them. By helping them develop a positive self-image, they will have the confidence needed to meet the demands of leadership. This is the definition of true youth empowerment.

Program planners should make every effort to ensure team activities allow each participant to experience some type of leadership role during the youth program.
For, example, serving in officer roles strengthens a participant's leadership capacity and reinforces leadership skills. If youth leaders are not given the opportunity to reinforce the skills learned they tend to forget them.

Effective youth leadership programs should focus on developing these four skill areas: social, interpersonal, behavioral and educational. This includes talking with the group members, listening to their ideas and concerns, and reading their reactions through non–verbal communications. Youth leaders should be given activities to learn and practice skills training in these categories as well: creativity, commitment, confidence, organization, ability to lead change, optimism, risk-taking, courage, strategic planning, social and self - awareness, and integrity.

Recruit Key Players
Recruit the right fit of volunteers and coordinators who will transform a youth leadership program from good to great! It takes the right volunteers and coordinators, who have a committed interest in youth leadership development, to help develop, plan, conduct and evaluate an empowering youth leadership program.

Determine the Budget
Financing a well- run youth leadership program is important. Time, material and resources all cost money. Some resources may be donated, such as a venue or people who volunteer to serve and train the youth. Typical funding needed can range from site rental fees to materials and supplies, as well as food for snacks and meals. These are just a few examples.

Some organizations do a fine job securing free resources through community agencies, schools or even the parents of the participants. If parents are invited to monitor the program, often they will volunteer to create a schedule for parent to donate snacks. A major expense typically includes the cost of developing the program and securing adequate trainers. Some church organizations employ youth pastors and staff, who might be available to conduct youth leadership training.

Don't neglect any opportunities to secure donations and apply for grants to cover some costs (See Appendix for sample of a budget).

Determine the Teaching Methods to be Used
Exposing youth leaders to quality leadership training requires diverse teaching techniques. Every youth leader responds differently. Remember, the greatest learning takes place when youth and adults see, hear and do what they are to learn Based on the ages of participants and length of the program, decide what methods to use when teaching various leadership topics. Common training methods include:
Group discussions, role playing, lecturing, group activities, multimedia presentations, experiential dyads (groups of 2) and trios (groups of 3) and teach-back sessions in which youth "teach back" to their peers what they have learned.

Determine Evaluation Strategy.
It is said that "what gets measured, gets done. And what gets recognized, gets done better!" Develop and conduct evaluations and surveys to assess the effectiveness of the program. What are the successes? What are the misses? What can be improved? What needs to be continued or stopped? The answers will determine if the objectives of the program were achieved.

There a variety of data collection methods available;
- Using a pre- and post-knowledge test before and after the training can help assess participants' understanding of leadership concepts.
- Self-assessments by participants are a direct and effective way to gauge how well the training was received and understood.
- Surveys to the teachers, trainers, volunteers, parents and other stakeholders will also provide important feedback on the program.
- Along with having a final evaluation of the program, planning a lessons-learned session amongst the trainers can provide valuable information to apply for future youth training events.

An effective evaluation process can help a program developer design repeatable and extraordinary youth programs that reinforce leadership skills and knowledge. This process can help answer the vital questions such as: What skills did the youth participants learn when they participated in the training program? How did they actually learn those skills?

One of the priorities should be to establish clear program goals and learning objectives, measure their effectiveness and track the progress made as a result of the leadership program.

Other Questions to Consider
Planning resources up front will maximize a program developer's opportunity to create an extraordinary youth leadership program. Sometimes the basic questions go unanswered during the initial planning of a youth program. Here are a few more questions relevant to strategizing and operating an effective youth leadership program:

What is the Time Frame?
Keeping youth leaders engaged in short periods of time is important. Be mindful of not only objectives and topics, but by the length of the activities and training sessions themselves. Don't overwhelm youth participants with too many topics in a short time. Strategically determine the appropriate time frame for each activity, session and duration of the program itself. Some programs can be more effective hosted as a continuous half-day (four hours) or full day (eight hours) session, while others may require hosting two hour sessions one day a week for to up six or eight weeks.

What is the Location?
It has been said that the key to setting up a good business is location, location, location. The same applies for selecting the location of a training program. Select a location that will create a safe and supportive learning environment. If use of a venue involves a rental cost, be sure to take that into consideration. Consider conducting the program at a school, which have rooms available for these types of activities.

How will the Training Program be Publicized?
Now that the program or session has been planned, publicizing the program is important to ensure maximum participation. If the program is for a specific school or organization, promotion efforts

may take place from within the organization. However, if it will be developed as a community-outreach program, parent-to-parent communication is an effective way encourage youth participant attendance. Other promotional methods may include the use of flyers, newsletters or print media, as well through social media platforms.

How Should the Program Conclude?
Youth leadership programs that are fun to participate in, and designed with recognition elements, often engage youth leaders the most. Bring the program to a close in a structured, well planned and celebratory manner. It gives the youth leaders and opportunity to celebrate their success with family and friends and to meet other community members with whom they can connect for community-service opportunities. Select a theme for the celebration. Develop an agenda that gives the youth participants an opportunity to demonstrate the skills they've learned. Additionally include prestigious speakers (a former program alumnus or other motivational keynote speaker).

Award youth leadership graduates with a certificate of completion that shows that the program was successful. A culmination ceremony is also the perfect vehicle for photo opportunities that later can be shared as memories, or even ways to promote future programs.

In general, people feel good about their achievements and receiving recognition. Conducting a culmination session sends the message to other youth leaders and parents that leadership development is an important value in their community.

TEAM ACTIVITIES THAT EMPOWER YOUTH LEADERS

Effective youth leadership programming involves creating team activities focused on teaching specific skills to youth leader that promote accountability, team work, collaboration and critical thinking. These are some of the key ingredients to engaging youth leaders and lay a strong foundation for them to adequately accept the responsibility of being empowered. These team activities should be developed with an orientation directed to achieve positive outcomes. While there are far too many activities to list here, it is important to note that activities should be hands-on and relevant. Here are just some basic activities to consider conducting to teach youth participants leadership principles in an engaging manner:

Leadership Awareness Activity:
1. In a larger group setting: Instruct participants to take 2-3 minutes to think about a leader who they know personally or have heard about (living or deceased).
2. Give them name tags and markers to write the names of their leader.
3. Instruct them to put on the nametags and introduce themselves to three other people in the room; as if they are the leader.
4. In the same group setting have participants give a characteristic or trait of their leader in one word. The trainer will record responses on a large poster board or butcher paper.
5. The trainer will ask students to provide descriptive examples of the characteristics and traits identified during the session. Additionally, trainers can point out words that reoccur.

Communication Activity:
1. Students will be divided into a straight line with five members in each group.
2. The trainer will communicate a short message or phrase into ear of the student at the front of the line.
3. Each student must repeat the message into the ear of the student beside him or her. The final person should repeat aloud to the group. Discuss any discrepancies or error and where the message breakdown occurred.
4. Rearrange and combine students into three larger groups and repeat step #2. Rearrange and combine students in one large group and repeat step #2.

How to Lead a Business Meeting
Leaders of any organization are busy people. For busy leaders, leading successful meetings requires having a set of rules in place when discussing important issues and planning activities. These kinds of rules promote that time management, an important element of conducting business efficiently.

Here are some solid tips for running a good meeting and helping participants in a youth program understand how to run meetings effectively.
1. Have an agenda. Prepare a written agenda for the meeting and distribute it to participants before the meeting.
2. Start and end the meeting on time. Every meeting should have a definite start and end time. Don't delay a meeting because not enough people have arrived. Start the meeting anyway to respect the time of those who did arrived early and on-time.
3. To keep meetings on track, follow the agenda. Don't let meetings drag on or get sidetracked by off-topic discussions. Encourage everyone to participate. No one person, including you, should dominate the discussion.
4. Make certain the meeting's purpose is accomplished. Then make sure everyone understands the decisions that were reached and any action that needs to be taken.

Empower Youth to Facilitate Group Meetings
Develop processes that empower youth leaders to elect group leaders or officers who will be accountable for the group's meetings and

activities. Many churches hold regular youth group meetings. Planning agendas and leading group meetings are typical responsibilities given to youth leaders in these groups. Consider implementing these officer roles into any youth leadership programs:

PRESIDENT:
- Presides over meetings.
- Responsible for planning and organization of meetings.
- Makes sure officers and participants are prepared.

VICE PRESIDENT:
- Assists president in program planning.
- Assumes duties of president if the president is absent.
- Acts as a timer for speech activities or to help trainer keep time on when facilitating a particular lesson plan.

SECRETARY:
- Keeps records of each meeting.
- Reads minutes of previous meetings.
- Assists trainer in keeping rolls, distributing materials, and communicating with group members.

LOGISTICS
- Is responsible for room set-up, equipment storage and preparation.
- Prepares the meeting place for each meeting.
- Is responsible for physical comfort of guests and members during the meetings (seating, lighting, etc.).
- Assists president in keeping order.

Practice How to Make Good Decisions
Good decisions come from disciplined thinking. Making good decisions takes practice and is habit forming. A positive attitude to life helps make major decision-making far easier and less stressful. Group discussions are effective ways to help youth leaders brainstorm and discuss characteristics that promote "good decision making."

Here are some suggestions, as recommended by Charles Foster, PhD of the Chestnut Hill Institute, in order to help youth leaders create discussion framework that facilitates good decision-making:

- Focus on the most important thing and keep things simple.
- Get what's needed to make a successful decision.
- Consider all options. Write down all positive and negative factors for and against taking a particular course of action
- Give up the notion that there is only one right solution to a problem/dilemma. Don't be afraid to make mistakes. Not making mistakes means you are not learning and growing.
- Stop and think before you act. Keep from doing the first thing that comes to mind!
- Get opinions and feedback from others you trust; but make the decision for yourself.
- Look for opportunities in any decision. Responsibility is not blame - don't blame others for your predicament.
- Change course if your strategy is not working. Learn when to change your direction if needed.
- Look ahead to the future - the past is already gone. See the path ahead as an adventure into the unknown and a time for challenge.

Mentoring Activity

Empowering youth leaders requires that they understand how to mentor others. Mentoring is more than merely teaching. It is more about sharing and guiding. Demonstrate to youth leaders how to mentor their peers. These suggestions highlight the importance of the mentor not doing the work for the mentee, but sharing ways of learning from personal experience and coaching.

The main aims of a peer mentor-mentee relationship are to:

- Recognize and identify the learning that has resulted from the personal experiences of the student in school and life.
- Develop a spirit of achievement by recognizing the skills used to overcome difficulties.
- Develop self-confidence and interpersonal skills of the students by allowing them to explore.
- Evaluate their own experiences of school life and to use it appropriately to help and guide younger or new students.
- Develop a sense of self-worth in acting as a peer mentor for other students.

How to Give an Organized Speech

Youth leaders must be able to communicate effectively if they are to voice their opinions and lead others. They must present ideas worth listening to and deliver their message with purpose and conviction. Suggest these four points to help empower them to communicate messages that will gain the attention of their audience and be of value to others.

- Decide instantly upon a clear and definite point-of-view on the subject. Then state it clearly.
- Prove the point of view with two or three specific reasons to support it.
- Give an example by sharing a personal experience or the experience of someone else to strengthen the point-of-view.
- Finish strong with a summary of the reasons you have given and present a call to action.

How to Actively Listen

Learning the importance of verbal and no-verbal communication helps youth leaders practice good listening skills. Here are some suggestions to help youth leaders practice becoming a good listener.

- Look the speaker in the eye.
- Sit attentively. Lean forward at times.
- Look as if you are enjoying listening. Raise your eyebrows, nod your head, smile, and laugh when appropriate.
- Ask questions.
- Make comments like , "I see" and "That's interesting," or "I never knew that."

How to Share Ideas

Learning to collaborate and share ideas are critical skills youth leaders will need. Most likely youth leaders will participate in group discussions. Sharing ideas effectively helps empowered youth leaders take ideas, suggestions and experiences and communicate them to others.

Discussion and the sharing of ideas is a customary method in leadership for solving problems, arriving at decisions or making plans. A good discussion is open and purposeful.

Here is a group activity to have youth leaders practice sharing ideas:

1. Break the class into three groups.
2. Give each group a problem to discuss and ask them determine a solution.
3. Each group will choose a group leader to serve as the spokesperson and a separate person to write down the ideas.
4. Have each group a) discuss the problem; b) discuss three possible solutions to solving the problem; and c) choose the best of the three solutions.
5. At the end, have the spokesperson of each group present their case. Ask them to state the problem they discussed, the three potential solutions and give the reason why the group chose that particular solution.

SUCCESS STORIES IN YOUTH LEADERSHIP

The following section is composed of success stories, testimonials and interviews on the benefits of youth leadership training from leaders of diverse backgrounds. These leaders all empower or have been empowered to be social change makers. Here are their stories.

EDUCATION: 100 YEARS AGO VS. TODAY IN THE 21ST CENTURY

We know each individual has a center of intelligence and an aptitude unique to them. Experience has shown that not everyone needs college right out of high school. There are exceptions to every rule. We don't send our kids to school to learn how to use a television remote. Most don't even read the instructions before assembling their toys. Instead, kids learn by doing. Yet, we want to send them to school to learn how to do what they love, and to help them figure out what they want to do when they grow up. The end result? We have retirees who still haven't figured out what they want to do when they grow up.

The paradigm I grew up with was, "above all get a good job, hope you can stay there for 40 years so you can get a hat or a gold watch, retire, then get in the box and let them throw dirt on you!" The problem is many people die with their dreams unfulfilled, never having tried to do that thing they always wondered and dreamed about.

Well surprise! Our kids are not having it. They are growing up with smartphones in their hands and learning how to do things we have told ourselves we are not good at.

I have a theory. Our youth need to get their hands on stuff so they can get a sense of what they are good at. They can figure out experientially what we've told them they need to learn about first. What are the 21st century principles and disciplines that address the challenges facing our youth today? First, it's important to have a good grasp of the concept of maps. A good map is a worthwhile tool in the right hands. It can show you where you are, where you can go and how to get there - if it's accurate. A map of Detroit, Michigan would not be a good map if you are in Los Angeles, California. No matter how accurate that Detroit map may be, it's only accurate for Detroit. It will not give you good directions in Los Angeles. You would need a map of Los Angeles to get around.

The same applies for the maps we are using for our youth leaders. We need to understand that the map adults are working with today is a map handed down to us by our parents, and in some cases our parent's parents or even our ancestors. It worked effectively in their eras. It worked for those in the industrial revolution, or even those in the 19th and 20th centuries who were training factory workers to conform to the factory rules. These maps don't apply to the 21st century because the rules, the technology, and the world experience has changed.

New, updated maps are needed to train the creators, entrepreneurs and rule changers of today. I've just stepped out of a 25+ year career as a cybersecurity professional. One of the complaints often heard about the educational background of the entry level candidates is universities are training youth with technology tools that are so…"yesterday". By the time these youth get into the workplace, the tools have changed and the rules have changed.

A perfect example of this change involves cyber professionals who trained employees to watch for and trust only websites showing the "Lock" icon preceding the URL. The lock icon indicated the site was using Secure Socket Layer (SSL) technology and encrypted. This was an easy way, in earlier days, to recognize if the information you submitted was secure, hence the site was legitimate. Well the evil ones (scammers) decided that they could buy SSL sites also and started setting up fake websites using SSL certificates. These had the "Lock" icon as well, but they were NOT secure. They were scam sites.

This was new information not being taught in the classrooms, nor on tests. The tests showed old information being scored as "correct," when in fact it was inaccurate. They persisted in using the old maps. Rules are changing so quickly that training folks in a classroom is simply not valid anymore. Our youth are getting second hand information and not being adequately prepared for the 21st century workplace.

One solution that has worked for certain industries is the use of interns. Providing youth with actual hands-on experience can bridge the gap between what's being taught in the college classroom versus what's happening in the real world. How do you train candidates in a technology that is evolving so quickly? In case you haven't been able to keep up, here is a shortlist of some of those technologies experiencing revolutionary and exponential growth: self-driving cars, drones, augmented reality, pervasive artificial intelligence in all areas of consumerism, quantum computing, deep fakes, ransomware, personal assistants with AI (think SIRI and ALEXA,) have become the norm today. These emerging technologies, uncontrolled by consumers, pose a threat to society, business, families, educational institutes and are rapidly becoming embedded in all areas of our lives.

In fact many segments of our communities, (think senior citizens) are considered to be digital immigrants (rather than digital natives like their grandkids). Seniors citizens, according to FBI statistics, were victimized to the tune of 37 billion dollars in losses due to scammer attacks in 2019 alone! This says that there is a growing need for "CyberSAFE" champions to help our aging population from being victimized.

What's the Solution?
Identifying the need for security – raising awareness in our communities of the opportunities for cyber awareness career roles and the need for cyber education. Training our youth with hands-on education can relieve the pressure valves of cyber bullying, cyber gangbanging, sexting, and illegal information sharing, password and identity theft. These cyber activities are occurring at epidemic proportions in our network neighborhoods.

Next, raise the awareness for needing to secure our services – With the growing presence of smart phones and intelligent assistants we need youth (and seniors) trained to help secure these devices. As the news headlines will attest, much of this new technology is not designed with security in mind and the end users need to know how to compensate for that lack of security by engaging their own human firewall. They need to know how to implement security best practices to keep themselves and their families safe. This is a new career opportunity in the making and a chance to create a whole new world for our youth wondering how to fit in the technology revolution.

Finally, knowledge of using the internet securely is a best practice that can result in recognition of scam websites and adoption of secure web surfing behaviors.

Since 2019 I have trained individuals to obtain a certification issued by Logical Operations and CertNEXUS, known as the CyberSAFE certification. Taught in a 3-to-4 hour class environment, it provides barebones level training customized for youth and adults alike, it is a low cost and hands-on class experience that results in a guaranteed certification. It sets youth end-user up for success. The amazing result of this certification is that it prepares youth for a career helping others to step into the world empowered as a cyber champion!

The really cool part about this is that it allows me to re-create my own success in this field in others. I started out helping others with their technology issues over 30 years ago because of my passion for service and extreme interest in understanding hackers and computer viruses. At that time the only thing we had to worry about were infected computer diskettes. Refrain from putting infected disks in your computer and voila! . . . you might be safe.

Fast forward to today, 30 years later. There are no more diskettes. Viruses have evolved into malicious software and the threats are coming at us from evil social engineers, calling us on the phone, hijacking our computers with popups and even taking over our Facebook and Instagram accounts!

My prediction? They will be taking over our ALEXA and security cameras (already done) our cars (already done), our credit profiles (already done) and our very lives. Who's watching YOUR computer devices? Who you gonna call? My invitation is for you to share this information with the youth in your life. Let's work together to build a national core of cyber champions empowered to support us all through this next wave of the technology revolution! Organizations, schools and community groups rely on computer end-users to understand and guard against the digital risks when using social media. Providers like Training Dynamics Network, which offers CyberSAFE End-user certified training, helps prepare technology-users against digital threats.

Training our youth leaders today and safe-guarding our youth's future, as well as our own, can protect our youth leaders of tomorrow against cyber attacks today - and in the 21st century.

- Michael B. Lattimore, Altadena, CA
Success Support, LLC

YOUTH LEADERSHIP IN ACTION!

After retiring from a 38 year career as an elementary school teacher with the Los Angeles Unified School District I knew I'd never go back to teaching. But fate had other plans. I had been a Toastmaster for five years when I discovered the Toastmasters Youth Leadership Program. Return to teaching? The lure proved irresistible.

With my wife's assistance, I began teaching a Youth Leadership Program at one of the Los Angeles South Region county parks. The experience has convinced me that youth leadership changes lives, because it works.

Dale and Rochelle's Stories
From that program, the memory of two students remain fresh in my mind. The first youth leader, let's call him Dale, was typical of a young person new to public speaking. At 15 or 16 years of age, he was shy, soft spoken, and, while speaking, seemed to find something on the floor more interesting than looking his audience.

During an eight week session he became a regular attendee. And he completed a speech or two, participated to a limited degree in table topics (the practice of speaking off the cuff) and giving evaluations. But Dale was never really comfortable speaking before an audience. None-the-less, he finish the eight week program. Despite his lack of confidence, however, Dale returned a year later for another session of the youth leadership program. And he had a story to tell.

During the time between sessions, he took the opportunity to go on an all-expenses paid trip to Europe and attend a program teaching young people about the World War II Holocaust. But first he had to qualify for the program, he explained, and that included passing a verbal interview. He shared with the interviewer he had participated in the Toastmasters Youth Leadership Program. It so happened, Dale said, that the interviewer was also a Toastmaster. Apparently, he felt that by being part of this extracurricular activity Dale had shown initiative and willingness to learn and grow. Dale qualified for the trip.

As you might guess, the trip was a milestone in Dale's life. Equally important, he learned to stand before an audience and share about his study of the Holocaust with notable skill. His eye contact had improved. His voice had power and range. His ability to engage an audience had grown substantially. In part, due to the seriousness of the trip and to his own maturation, his confidence and skill in speaking before an audience had grown. I'm also convinced that his time in the Toastmasters Youth Leadership Program had helped polish his public speaking skills.

Then there was Rochelle. Rochelle was a teenage girl whose Toastmaster journey story also involved a trip. Unlike Dale, she was more comfortable on stage. She had spent time in the youth leadership program polishing her skills and building her confidence. During her early high school years, she and other young ladies were blessed with the opportunity to visit the White House and met the former first lady, Michelle Obama. During that visit, Rochelle explained, the group was asked to choose a spokesperson. Having participated in the Toastmasters Youth Leadership Program she felt comfortable speaking before an audience. Rochelle volunteered, which led to an incredible journey for her.

I have not resumed my teaching career. However, as you might guess, seeing these young people grow through youth leadership was a feel good moment for me, my wife and the staff of the South Region Los Angeles County Parks; a feeling just as satisfying as my 38 years in teaching.

- **Everette Williams,** Los Angeles, CA
Retired Teacher

PROJECT-BASED LEARNING IN A 21ST CENTURY SCHOOL

In the Beginning

I was a brand new principal during year one of the newly opened "21st Century School." When folks ask me how long I've been at Fort Worthington Elementary, I jokingly say, and it is true, 'I came with the building.' I was recruited by one of the best instructional leadership executive directors (ILED) I've ever known.

Previously I was serving in a leadership capacity at an international baccalaureate school, a K-3 section of a larger school with 250 children. As a parent of two children, who also attended the school, I knew every child and their parents by name, served on the family council and was an active PTA parent as well. Did I mention the school was seven minutes by car from my home? Yes, I was comfortable.

The ILED disrupted my comfortable setting by offering me the opportunity to become principal of a low performing school, in the heart of East Baltimore, which had been housed in a swing space for two years. The school's population was 444, besieged by poor performance on the statewide assessment, 158 suspensions and was essentially what educators colloquially describe as a school "on fire."

The school was moved into a 21st century building in August 2017. Receiving an investment of $37,000,000, the school district outfitted the facility with the latest technology. I accepted the challenge.

After being appointed the new principal of Fort Worthington Elementary Middle School over the summer, I engaged in fact finding interviews and connection sessions with teachers, staff, children and family members. I thought these meetings would provide me with data on logistics, insight into culture, who had informal authority and resources to infuse purpose, healing, and empowerment.

I found that empowerment, purpose and project-based learning initiatives were key elements needed to transform this new school, its community and its culture. We immediately partnered with the Holistic Life Foundation to develop a mindful moment room, staffed with a full time yogi to facilitate individual, group and class sessions on mindfulness and yoga. We also partnered with AKOBEN, to educate us on restorative practices, use of affective language, the social discipline window and connection.

In order to establish purpose, I facilitated healing circles with the staff, providing them with the opportunity to practice visioning, share stories of triumph and pain and connect with each other on a deeper level. This practice has now become the basis for what teachers do with scholars at the beginning of the day and the beginning of every class period for content teachers. These mindfulness practices have created a nurturing and loving family environment that has high expectations.

With experience serving as a teacher in a startup transformational school for four years, and being trained by new leaders" I knew what needed to happen. We needed to find purpose and answer the relevant questions: Why are we here? What are we here to do? What drives our decision making? What's best for our children? Simply put, we needed a vision to ground our work in.

Seeing is Believing
Fort Worthington Elementary Middle School is now affectionately known as "The Fort," a school with the vision of academic excellence. Its vision statement is:

> *At The Fort we exude growth and excellence at all times, through positivity and collaboration with staff, scholars, and the community; ensuring accountability and achievement for all!*

This vision was developed through a shared decision making process and is one of the components of process project-based learning. Three stakeholder groups (staff, scholars, and families) engaged in the facilitative leadership session titled, *Open, Narrow and Close Protocol* to identify the main ingredients that make up their ideal school.

After an analysis and coding of all of the lists, the instructional leadership team at The Fort identified the common themes of excellence, continued growth, human connection through relationship building, achievement, and accountability.

Project Based Learning Initiative
Project-based learning was our catalyst to actualize our vision, empower scholar voice, meet the varied needs of our scholars, and provide our teachers with the opportunity to grow professionally while facilitating children to be leaders of their own learning.

Using the Buck Institute's *Gold Standard of Project-Based Learning*, we began the planning for four cycles of Project-Based Learning (PBL), for grades K - 8. Our approach to PBL was organic and aligned to our beliefs as a school. We believe in the village concept, that each individual is responsible for the collective. This belief is grounded in our restorative practices initiative.

Since empowerment and experiential learning were key components of the rubric, we created opportunities for students to create project topics that were aligned to social change in their community.

This authentic, experiential approach tapped into our scholars' moral impetus, thereby motivating them to do their very best. Project based learning provides opportunities for our youth to decide the path they want to take to approaching their inquiry or solving their problem.

One example of this is our fall festival. Our middle schoolers discussed the problem of scholars' lack of engagement in school. They posed the question, "How can we make learning more engaging and fun while maintaining its rigor?"

Scholars developed a myriad of approaches to this question. The end result was a fall festival in which they engaged their K - 5 peers in learning games aligned to the Common Core State Standards. This project required students to:

- Engage in research of grade appropriate tasks for their participants,
- Collaborate to develop stations that were interactive and standards aligned,
- Demonstrate creativity, and
- Communicate with each other effectively and purposefully.

Scholars then used the funds from the concessions to fund their community garden plan. By the way, the community garden is now home to over 35 different crops, planted, cultivated, and harvested by our very own scholars. Our projects increase engagement between elementary and middle schoolers, but also put the learning in the hands of our scholars (A video of our Project-Based Learning Initiative can be found at www. vimeo.com/cityschools/fallfestival).

Project-based learning has truly tapped into our scholars' multiple learning modalities. Our PBLs helps the community. Our community garden has provided fresh produce for community members who have to travel more than a mile to the nearest market.

Our PBLs help our students. Their needs are being met and folks are actually listening to them, allowing them to make choices. They are empowered to lead and advocate for their needs. This social change has also encouraged them to think of the collective, thereby, creating a positive learning environment for scholars where they feel safe to take risks.

(The following is an excerpt from 2018-2019 Work Plan Co-developed by Dawn Shirey, Director of 21st Century Learning and school leadership teams.)

The professional learning occurring on the early release days will address how to motivate students; increase students' understanding of concepts and ability to apply these concepts to real-life situations; teach students how to work in a team; and build students' critical thinking, communication, and problem solving skills through the implementation of Project Based Learning.

To meet the student needs identified above, teachers need to be able to:

- **Create or adapt projects** for students and plan for implementation of the project from the launch to the culminating activity.
- **Promote student independence and growth,** open-ended inquiry, team spirit, and attention to quality throughout project implementation.
- **Use formative and summative assessments of knowledge, understanding, and success skills, and include self and peer assessment** of team and individual work.
- Engage in learning and creating alongside students, and **identify when students need skill-building, redirection, encouragement, and celebration.**

- **Monique Debi,** Baltimore, MD
Principal, Fort Worthington Middle School

TEACHING LEADERSHIP IN THE KITCHEN

The Detroit Food Academy (DFA) is a 501(c)(3) organization that works to inspire young Detroiters (ages 10-24) through culinary arts and food entrepreneurship. Through this process, they grow as holistic leaders who are healthy, connected and powerful to effect change in our communities and beyond.

In a brief telephone interview in September 2019, Co-founder and Executive Director Jen Rusciano expounded on the program as it relates to the EMPOWER concept. DFA employs two concepts called The Triple Bottom Line. (People, Planet and Profit!) and the Achieve-Connect-Thrive (ACT). The triple bottom line is an accounting framework with three parts: social, environmental and financial. (Some organizations have adopted the TBL framework to evaluate their performance in a broader perspective to create greater business value.)

Why do you think youth leadership and what DFA does is important?

Rusciano: Like youth leadership, DFA helps young leaders to know what they are and what they are not. Our program gives them variety to learn different things. The key is to help kids break through it all.

Why does DFA use the "Triple Bottom Line and ACT processes and how do they apply to the DFA program for young people?

Rusciano: They are borrowed concepts we use as these are concepts and processes proven to work. Every business has a triple bottom line. It is a common business concept for social, environmental and financial aspects of any business. [Our process] is aligned with the core values of leadership. It digs deep and touches the heart of helping our young people. It helps the schools, the community and families alike. It's the engaging part, which is the hook. It gets their attention and they go through the journey. The work we do creates both sides of the solution - the hook and the journey. Young people want to see what works and how it works.

Are there challenges youth face while going through the DFA?

Rusciano: Sure there are challenges before and after school. One major challenge can be transportation issues. What is important is the partnership with the community and parents as well . . . helping them overcome the challenges of getting to the program. Some of these kids in Detroit have to start leaving their house at 4:30am, when it is dark and sometimes cold during the winter times. Some have to take 2-3 busses to get to the downtown area of Detroit for school. We need to help them. They need the community's help. They need our voice.

How do those who have completed the program help? Do they help with the students learning communication as part of the programs?

Rusciano: The coordinator role does an awesome job to help our youth. We have people who have gone through the program and some of the advanced participants helping the youth. In the Food Entrepreneur project students learn to pitch their business. Some times we have to focus just on the basic communication skills. Just to get a young person to stand up and speak in front of their peers can be a challenge.

Is the main focus just helping young people start their own food business?

Rusciano: No. Some of them (youth) don't like the food culinary business necessarily but they like the leadership part. It's not solely about just getting them to start a business in the food industry. They are empowered to learn what works for them. What works for one youth may not work for another.

What about the community partnerships and school-based programs, how do help the youth?

Jen: These youth often need help. They need the community and the parents. We talk about leadership, vision and how to support each other. We have that type of dialogue with everyone. There are teachers and community people who teach them about everything from writing cover letters to doing taxes. The school-based program helps teach them be accountable, to call someone if they're running late and how to solve challenges to their issues. We are the connection for them to resources and people who can help them learn. It's about looking at and treating them as individuals. We help them to have personal goals and to be able to reach those personal goals. We let them know 'If you are excited about the food business and are passionate, we have people we can connect you to in the industry.

If you had to choose just two elements that are vital to leadership, what would they be?

Rusciano: Experiential and empowerment would be the two core ingredients. Those are the project-based learning parts. The young people are learning to make their own responsible choices. They decide on the budget, they decide the discussion points. And, some of our coordinators are graduates of the program, who come back to work with other youth. It's youth helping other youth.

Q: Many times our young people are afraid of failure. What is DFA's perception on failing?

Jen: We make it OK to fail in our classes. It is about having balance in life. Youth live in a world (on social media, television) where they see cooking shows and see only the finished products. They only see the best of people's lives, the "best" scenarios. They don't often see the behind the scenes part. When a kid enters our program and starts cutting up carrots, and the carrot is not cut up right or looks like what they've seen on TV they are discouraged. They say 'I'm bad at this.' They flip over the cutting board and want to quit. We have to dial it back a bit and reinforce that what they see on TV took time . . . that those chefs have practiced over and over again, through hours and hours. We have to show them it is OK . . .that failing is part of the learning part. We have to remind them it is a process. It is easy not to try. It takes walking through the mud, so to speak, to finish the race. A lot of people never even enter the race.

Interview with Jen Rusciano, Detroit, MI
Co-Founder and Director,
Detroit Food Academy

COMMUNICATION AND LEADERSHIP IN THE KITCHEN

Whenever I see or hear people watch or talk about sports teams, I often wonder why they don't share the same enthusiasm when it comes to food establishments. Yes, there are those who call themselves 'foodies' who obsess about food, but overall the way people talk about food pales in comparison to the way they talk about or interact with sports.

The gap is getting closer though with most of the FoodTV® Network shows resembling sports events. When the FoodTV® Network first got established back on April 19, 1993, there was only one show in the food competition category (*Ready... Set... Cook!*). The rest of the shows were either news segments (*In Food Today with David Rosengarten and Donna Hanover*) or instructional videos. Now, most, if not all, of the shows on this network are game shows.

In spite of that, most people would instinctively rather pay hundreds of dollars to watch a sporting event over paying the same amount to enjoy a true fine dining experience even though at the core of it all, there are countless similarities between the two encounters. These shows promote teamwork, development of communication skills, decisive actions and sense of self-esteem, community and time management. Today, even our youth leaders are getting in on the game. I say, let's enlarge the kitchens of all restaurants. Build seats around the entire kitchen and open it up for people to cheer on their favorite kitchen teams to complete an entire meal to victory. After all, it takes a great team to execute a flawless, picture perfect and flavor-packed meal - dish after dish. I remember when I used to work as a prep cook for a small restaurant near our home, the kitchen was very small and it was tight having four people in it to prepare and complete meals for all the tickets coming in. There would be nights where we would get 'slammed' but we managed to send food out with little to no complaints. It seems that we were cooking one for the Gipper.

We had a lead cook manning the range, griddle, grill, and frying stations (referred to as the line); another cook on the appetizer and salads station that also took charge of the line when the lead cook had to step away; me on the prep table to assist with salads, appetizers, desserts, and prepping the ingredients for the line; and a dishwasher (person). Each individual reached out to the rest of the team if they needed something and the others would respond by providing and meeting the needs without question. We all knew that we had a goal to fulfill each order in a timely manner at the best quality and we all knew that we had to do this consistently. These are the same intentions and attitude that are common to each sports team. Wait a minute. What would it look like to combine communication and leadership with expert culinary skills in a fast competitive environment? Let me share my vision on what this environment might sound like. I'll call it The Amazing Food Race!

Welcome to The Amazing Food Race Restaurant
Imagine this scenario. You and your family go out to dine at your favorite restaurant. You are led to the third row of comfortable cushioned bleachers, along with other diners. You find yourself in the center of an arena style restaurant, directly facing a kitchen stadium.
Everyone is seated. The lights dim. An explosion of fanfare and lights fill the dining room of the restaurant. The announcers, Pat Summers and Jim Buick, arrive and begin their introductions, coming in loud and clear over the arena speakers:

Pat Summers: Good evening ladies and gentlemen, and welcome to the Four Seasons Stadium. It's a great evening for fine dining; not a cloud in the ceiling… This is Pat Summers and with me is Jim Buick. So Jim, what's your prediction on tonight's meal service outcome?

Jim Buick: Well Pat, you can't get a job without experience and you can't get experience until you have a job. Once you solve that problem you are home free. I gotta say though, tonight's head chef, Jean-Claude, has a great track record. He started his career as a dishwasher at Gourmet Conspiracy and worked his way to head chef after being traded throughout the big leagues during lamb season.

Pat Summers: The team enters the kitchen area. The crowd goes wild. The first food ticket of the night is handed to the expediter. He calls out the order to the staff and the game begins… Mario Valenti grabs a healthy handful of greens and tosses them into his bowl.

Jim Buick: Pat, you know that there's a 15-minute window that the salad needs to go out into the dining floor, so Jean-Claude has got to be careful not to start his protein too soon… although with his current stats, there's only a 19.5 percent chance of that happening.

Pat Summers: I don't doubt that Jean-Claude will perform less than perfect tonight. He appears to be at the top of his game… wait, there seems to be some commotion going on in the kitchen. Let's go to our man on the floor, Dick Myers, to see what's happening.

Dick Myers: Pat, it seems that one of the pans that Jean-Claude was handed still had a residue of the last protein. This lack of attention to details is unfortunate because it'll cost the team a 2-3 minute delay. This is a technical foul on Kenny Jensen, their dishwasher. This will be Kenny's third penalty during the season. One more and I'm afraid he will be out the door. Back to you, Pat.

Pat Summers: Such a shame as it's not that easy to find a good dishwasher in the league… 10 minutes into the game, Jean-Claude dribbles the meat between his hands and lays it in the searing hot pan. Beautiful execution by Jean-Claude.

Jim Buick: Yes, and a great save by Kenny with a second clean pan. Wow! How did he pull that one off?!

Pat Summers: Horacio Sanchez follows up with the sides and garnish. Mario just called out 'salad at the window!' That means that Jean-Claude and Horacio have about 10-15 minutes to complete the main entrée and get it out to the dining room floor. Any longer than that and the dining fans get a little irritable.

Jim Buick: That's what happened during Super Bowl 2002. James Emery, the head chef at the Boston Dinery fumbled the meal and it cost them the main course. The service took too long and the dining fans just started walking out.

Pat Summers: When the fans expect a perfect meal, you can't serve hamburgers in place of a porterhouse steak. Well, it looks like they are nearing the end of the service and are about to put the dish up to the window. Horacio plates the sides and hands it off to Jean-Claude for the protein... Jean-Claude carefully places the protein on top of the starch and legumes... Nice! He drizzles the demi-glaze on the plate below the protein and pipes the contrasting raspberry sauce with the squeeze bottle... Horacio with the assist on the garnish and sends the completed dish to the window... GOAAAAAAAAAAL! The crowd is going wild! They have never experienced such a memorable amalgamation of flavors in such an exciting gastronomic event!

Pat Summers: Well, Jim, that's the end of another culinary artistry and it's time to partake of the team's efforts.

Jim Buick: Yes!. Jean-Claude certainly pulled it off again with such a graceful execution on cooking the protein to perfection. All in all, my hats off to the entire team for a great service. They wouldn't have pulled out this third win without their fantastic teamwork and communication. That ranks them second in the division behind the Lafayette Bistro. I just hope that the division takes compassion on Kenny and gives him another chance. I'd hate to see Four Seasons lose such a great dishwasher.

Pat Summers: On behalf of Four Seasons Stadium, thank you for dining with us tonight. Until the next event, this is Pat Summers and Jim Buick wishing you a great evening.

[The above story is fictional. Any references to names of actual persons or businesses are purely coincidental.]

- **Sam Paano,** Lakewood, CA.
Gourmet Conspiracy

FROM YOUTH LEADERSHIP TO BILLIONAIRE BURGERS

Sometimes I would just stand in front of that food truck, gazing at the name in big red letters, thinking to myself, "Cool. The Billionaire Burger Boyz. Not too bad!" There were many things I learned through my experiences with youth leadership. The cooking business, though, is my thing!

I can't recall all the reasons that led me into so many youth leadership activities and don't recall all youth leadership workshops I participated in. These days I use my leadership skills to keep up with opening up the shop, handling payroll, catering events and staying on top of my social media marketing for my food business with partner Chef Soulo. Yeah, I grew up learning some great public speaking skills, but cooking has always been my thing.

As a kid my mom and dad put me in baseball. I really wanted to play football but I guess they had this fear of me getting hurt. It didn't matter though, because when I reached Paramount High School I played varsity football all three years, was a team captain and won MVP my senior year.

When I was 9 or 10 years old, my dad would drag me with him to his Toastmasters meetings. He would participate in the meetings, while I sat in the back, quietly doing my homework. One year the group suggested I participate in what they called table topics, where you would answer an impromptu question in one to two minutes. Out of five adults who participated, I was awarded a ribbon for the "Best Table Topics Speaker." Everyone smiled, clapped (they clapped a lot) and was so proud. I think they found out I was actually paying attention to the meetings. "Wow," I thought, "I beat the adults?" For some reason, though, they never really asked me to participate again.

Over the next five years, I started participating in Toastmasters Youth Leadership. I learned how to structure a speech with passion, stories and a strong message. Through middle and high school I was winning youth speech contests and serving in leadership and emcee roles for teacher and student events. I guess I could be considered a paid speaker too, having been awarded cash scholarships for winning first place in the Annual Firecrackers Toastmaster Youth Competition and in the Paramount District Rotary Club Youth Competition. By 18, I began to organize and facilitate youth leadership workshops, guiding other kids on how to prepare speeches and lead group discussions.

Youth Leadership training really helps young people become excellent communicators and leaders, and helps them become more confident. For me, I believe learning to communicate a clear message and leading others helped me find success. Employment interviews and landing jobs seemed to come easy. Having a command of great communication skills allowed me to do very well in getting promoted to leadership positions at jobs. By 21 years old I felt motivated, empowered and confident toward working on my dreams to have my own business, and show other young people how to do the same. That day soon came true.

At 22, I traded in my motivational speaking skills for a spatula and a grill and launched my first business as Chef Smokehouse Lee. My parents still have pictures of me cooking my first burger when I was four years old and mastering the bar-b-que grill at seven. Cooking has always been my passion. Thank goodness for leadership skills.

With a vision, a mission, and my Uncle Melvin's customized 15-foot barbeque trailer grill, I began cooking and "selling my dream." My team-building skills helped me muster up a team to help me run the barbeque catering business. Not being at a loss for words or competing I gained notoriety in the barbeque business.

Within a few months I talked my way into competing in cooking competitions hosted by sponsors like the HavasuBrew BBQ and the Kansas City Barbecue Society (KCBS). One of my proudest moments was capturing 3rd Place at the KCBS Competition at the Santa Anita Race Track. At 23, I thought I had found my ultimate business niche; until I met Chef Soulo and his girlfriend Jennifer.

Two years later, with a food truck and a vision, I became co-owner and chief operations officer of the Billionaire Burger Boyz, LLC. And now, after running 2 food trucks, appearing on food network shows, winning two TV cooking competitions, receiving a proclamation from the City of Los Angeles for organizing community events and presently owning a fast food brick-and- mortar restaurant, I have come to believe it all began with youth leadership.

My vision to build an enterprise that teaches other young people how to start their own business is stronger now than ever. I feel empowered to make my own decisions, motivated to pursue my dreams, recognized by the countless customers who eat and enjoy our food. Every chance I get, I tell young people to invest in themselves, work hard and practice their communication and leadership skills they need to bring their dreams to life.

Every chance I get I spend time using their communication skills talking to our forty-three (43) thousand followers on Instagram about coming to the shop and "getting their issue" of huge gourmet burgers and my signature *jambalaya fries*. I feel I have I found my voice and my passion, telling customers, "You don't have to be a billionaire to eat like one . . . get in theeeerre!"

- **Davidlee Kitchen,** Cypress, CA
Billionaire Burger Boyz, LLC

YOUTH RECOGNITION IN THE REFINERIES

Back in my days as a teenager, most of my world consisted of playing video games like Nintendo, Galaga and even Pac-Man (for us boomers). The main recognition I was looking for was getting to the next level in the game, so I could best my friends. To our youth today, recognition is still important. Recognition works in communication and leadership just the same as with video games that motivate, inspire and challenge them.

As a member of Toastmasters International, my club, Refined Speakers Toastmasters, has had the privilege over the past ten years to support our host refinery's summer youth program for the past 20 years. The mission of the program is to provide real industrial summer jobs for youth in the neighboring high schools surrounding the refinery. The program selects 35 to 50 participants for the program from the 200+ applications received from targeted high schools.

As part of the youth seven week education, students learn work skills, the discipline of showing up to work on time every day, and working as a part of diverse teams. They learn soft skills, planning their day for success, creating a resume, participating in interviews with other companies, and public speaking training. For six weeks the students are broken down into groups of four to seven. Meetings are moderated by one or two leaders from the Toastmasters Club. Each week the students would deliver a four to six minute speech on topics of their

choosing, with a focus on honing a specific skill in speech organization, speech evaluation, gestures, vocal variety and presenting for impact
The greatest impact on the youth are moments when the reward for *Best Speaker* is selected by student votes. Nothing stirs up excitement more than when the best speaker are announced with much fanfare, to rousing cheers from the youth and adults alike.

Over the years we used a number of different means to recognize weekly winners. We have used ribbons, custom made printed certificates and handmade traveling trophies consisting of mason jars filled with chocolates and mints. The winner for a given week could consume the sweets with their friends and attach some meaningful item on the jar. Some placed a sticker with their school's name or favorite sports team, a label, a ribbon, a handmade yarn bracelet or anything else of meaning. The students were extremely proud of these awards and proudly displayed them on their Summer Youth Program notebooks.

We discovered over the years that it really did not matter what we provided as the recognition vehicle. Any recognition item seemed to impact student behavior and performance. Additionally, at the end of the program, students who won the Best Speaker and Most Improved Speaker awards would be given custom designed trophies to recognize their accomplishments at their program graduation.

Why does recognition work to drive our youth performance? Well, there are a number of factors:

Encouragement
Because of the target schools involved in the program, the group's demographics are quite diverse. Students come from all walks of the education spectrum; from typical neighborhood high schools and high performing top students to leading math and science academies, as well as continuation students working through life's challenges.

Overall, a significant number of students come from at-risk situations, stigmatized from lack of self-esteem and little confidence. Recognition makes them feel successful and encourages them to keep doing their best. The recognition and encouragement they received during the course of the program, provides a boost in self-esteem, giving them all positive mindsets to understand that they could do better and improve themselves even beyond the program.

Confidence
Fear of public speaking is commonly considered as a top three fear for many people. We instill in the youth that the more they practice public speaking skills, the better they will become at delivering presentations. Learning speaking techniques gives them the opportunity to share their experiences, which helps improve their self-esteem and confidence significantly. Students surveyed at the end of our program consistently indicate their confidence skyrocketed after receiving special recognition. Furthermore, recognition of their efforts served as a catalyst which helped increase confidence and ultimately performance.

Competitive Energy
It provides a competitive edge for our youth. Observing others perform weekly roles and delivering speeches effectively prompted the youth to summon and lean on their internal competitiveness to get their work done. Many of them did not think they could muster up the skill to speak in front of other people at the beginning of the program. Being recognized publicly for their performances instills a greater sense of urgency, driving all of them to better performance.

Recognition Works.
Properly administered recognition programs motivate youth leaders to perform at their highest levels. The reward or token of appreciation does not have to be major or costly. The value of recognition is intrinsic. Even a small token that has very low actual financial value can spark a sense of appreciation, confidence and competitiveness. .

The true value is based on what it represents to the recipient. Adults are in the unique position of being able to change the trajectory of the life of a youth. Recognition is one of the key components any youth organization can employ to fully engage our youth leaders. Let's stand up, step out and make a difference today!

- **Keith Jackson,** Chino Hills, CA
ETEC Consulting, LLC

DISCOVERING ENGAGEMENT AND LEADERSHIP RESPECT

I am a youth ministry evangelist and oversee youth groups. My experience has shown me that while young people want to learn leadership, not every young person wants to be a leader. While working the youth I found that they want to be respected, not ordered or bossed around like a puppy. I recognized they wanted their opinions, ideas and concerns heard. They wanted to have a say in things that involved them at church.

When I was nominated to be the youth director at my church, I accepted. I was hoping to set an example for my children first and foremost. I wanted them to be leaders not followers. Young people have many friends and I want them to be influencers rather than followers.

My youth department had something to prove. So did I. The youth ages ranged from 7 to -16 ½ years old. When the teenagers were told to do something at the church, they were talked to in an overbearing manner.

The teenagers would resist, with an attitude of indifference. The adults had attitudes. The teenagers had the same attitudes. Neither side budged and therefore neither group was communicating with each other well. When I defended the youth, that's when it was decided that I would oversee the youth by being the youth director. I changed everything. Their goal was to show the adults that they are reliable and capable of demonstrating self-control and intelligence. Personally, I needed to show the adult departments that adults can communicate with children, especially the teenagers, without treating them as if they didn't matter.

Under my direction, the youth elected officers for the youth department. The offices elected were president, vice president, secretary, treasurer and sergeant at arms. The president was 16 or 17 at the time. The Treasurer was eleven years old and was responsible for training his assistant, who was nine years old. Serving in these roles, our youth group learned accountability and teamwork. When someone was reluctant to take on a leadership role, they felt someone had to step up and volunteered. So, each one did. The youth felt empowered.

After adequate training and spending a little time settling in their roles, they committed to and planned youth Sundays. The youth leaders planned who would conduct the announcements, what songs would be sung and who would sing, and what "unity" colors (attire) they would wear. They were in charge of their fundraisers. They were empowered to decide their field trip locations: Magic Mountain, Soak City and so on.

When our church fellowshipped for youth Sundays at other churches, they encouraged each other to do their best. Don't get me wrong, they did have issues among each other. In those instances, I would give them the opportunity to work through their challenges or problems. As the youth director, I helped guide them through conflict-resolution to help them with problem solving. It slowly became evident that these young people, after being placed in leadership roles, were doing quite well. Their confidence and self-respect increased. They were in charge of making responsible decision for themselves and the lives of other youth at the church.

Before developing the youth department, the adult parishioners were accustomed to bossing the youth around, not allowing them to make decisions or do anything unless instructed by the adults. No one knew how to speak or communicate with each other. After the changes I implemented, the adults were still overbearing. They questioned everything, even my authority and permission for the youth decisions.

I learned that sometimes change needs to be modified as well. To ease the adult department feeling of not being in control. I decided it was best if I personally addressed any issues on behalf of the youth department. I would then communicate the wishes of the adult department to the youth group. I learned a thing or two during this process.

While my intervening on behalf of the youth group seemed to work for a while, I found out that apparently some of the young leaders in the youth department did not want to be leaders. The president of the youth department really didn't enjoy being the leader. It became apparent that serving in that leadership role just wasn't for him. He said he merely decided to give it a try for me. He was comfortable, he said, with just being on the team.

I began to realize that respect and empowerment was the real driving force of the new youth department. Suddenly, what made it acceptable for them was that everything was okay as long as I was always guiding the group. They just wanted an adult to show that the youth group mattered. They understood their role, as young people, was to always be respectful to anyone, particularly to any adult. What they really wanted was to be treated with a little concern and respect.

- **Michelle King,** Long Beach, CA
Power Praise Ministries

EMPOWERMENT THROUGH OPTIMISM

Project Optimism is a nonprofit organization in Sacramento, California that was started by Armoni Easley and Ishmael Pruitt. Both are California natives and during their own childhood witnessed multiple individuals within their community and family fall to oppressive systemic forces: substance abuse, prison, poverty and gangs.

The goal of Project Optimism is to provide programs and events that inspire optimistic mindsets in individuals, with an emphasis on youth and young adults. This is done through what is called the Sankofa Project. Me'Lisa James (also a California native) and Justin Maclin, who are involved with Project Optimism, shared their feelings about leadership among young people and how it relates to Project Optimism. Justin also took the opportunity to ask Founder Armoni Easley questions about the program and how it relates to empowering youth leaders.

How does Project Optimism relate to youth leadership and how does it work?

Maclin: Project Optimism is more than just the name of an organization. It's a movement that structures young people's passions and their way of life. The young leaders who are involved with the organization are usually students who attend colleges in the Sacramento Area. These young leaders are in search of opportunities to change and uplift their communities while evolving into future leaders and decision makers. This comes in the form of what the company calls the Sankofa Project. Sankofa is a Ghanaian phrase for "go back and get."

How does the Sankofa Project work?

Maclin: The Sankofa Project fully engages youth leaders as a free mentorship program for middle and high school students in Sacramento neighborhoods. Youth are matched up with mentors (college students and young professionals) The Sankofa Project experience provides youth with the support and direction needed to develop as committed learners ready to contribute to the world. The Sankofa Project creates an extended support system that enhances students' academic achievement and social, emotional and physical wellbeing.

What are the expectations of the project? How are youth empowered?

Maclin: There are a number of anticipated outcomes for the Sankofa Project mentees:
- To improve students' self-esteem, resiliency, problem-solving, anger management, mental health and create for themselves hope for the future.
- To improve in academics and social skills; to decrease chronic truancies and absences, suspensions and expulsion, and eliminate high-risk behaviors: fights, drugs, gangs, etc.

Me'lisa James and Armoni Easley statements about Project Optimism:

How does Project Optimism engage or empower the youth?

James & Easley : Engagement is the key. We have found that our success is based on our own experiences. The bottom-line question is: How are we helping the youth involved in the program to become good people? Also, what happens when things don't go right?

We have learned new ways to relate and encourage youth to help them feel empowered and believe in themselves. As the current directors, we have found through our past experiences working in the classroom and with counseling organizations that engaging youth in supplementary programs is a unique skill. The Sankofa Project typically runs on the weekends or during after-school hours. We seemed to have found the right engagement formula that encourages youth participants to consistently attend our program and outings.

We have found that to empower youth there must be authenticity and trust. Youth can tell when you are trying to hold power and authority over them. It is important for adults and directors to be willing to take a step back and become open to learning from youth.

Who helps to work with the youth? Who oversees the project?

James: We are all here to help. In our workshops everyone is on the same level. We start with the idea that some of us are older with more life experience, but at the end of the day we are all the same. We are all doing our best to be good people and keep moving forward. Life does not always get easier, but if you have the right mindset, you will always progress. Knowing this and having the right community to support you allows empowerment to flourish in youth.

What are the ultimate learning points for the youth?

Maclin: The key to successful youth leadership and growth is to allow youth the opportunity to create what they feel the program should look like, based on what Project Optimism stands for. We all want to find a way to help young people be leaders. Many times, however, they are already leaders. They just need an environment that allows them to show those leadership skills, and a knowledgeable curriculum that ensures they put those good leadership skills to great use. This is where opportunity meets change when dealing with the youth today through Project Optimism.

- Justin Maclin & Me'Lisa James, Sacramento, CA
Project Optimism, Inc.

YOUTH LEADERSHIP LEADS TO ENTREPRENEURIAL DREAMS

People have said that I have a camera- friendly face and bright smile, but I am more comfortable behind the scenes directing and producing. For this reason I am proud of being a young entrepreneur and a producer in this digital age of social media.

Since I was perhaps three years old I have always fallen in love with the arts over and over again. I grew up watching films and shows like *A Different World*, *Moesha*, *Martin*, and *The Wiz* just to name a few. Much of my ambitions did not come to life from any particular youth leadership club or program. I had participated in some youth leadership programs and saw the unlimited opportunity to learn leadership and potentially be a change agent in the world, promoting equality and justice in the world. Participating in leadership programs helped give me a voice to bring to light cultural awareness and social change.

I have always believed in being my own person, all through middle school. But it was my leadership exploration in high school that took my passion for leadership to new heights. This is where I began to understand youth empowerment and my purpose for helping people. I leaped into student government, helping to organize student activities on campus involving theater and social gatherings. Being involved in student government gave me the opportunity to launch the school's first African American Culture Club.

After graduating from high school and leaving California to attend Bennett College in North Carolina, I found my true calling. Because of my deep infatuation with the arts I thrived in my quest to learn more about media studies. In college, I got involved in theatre, took on an internship with Radio KJLH and joined the Journalism Honors Society.

Then it happened. It was at Bennett College where I created a web talk-show *College Daze*, and filmed my first documentary, *Who You Calling a B*tch?*, studying the psychological effects of reality television. This all led to my expanding the College Daze brand into my own social media company and producing a documentary series called *23 & Graduated*, and my greatest personal accomplishment: an animation series called *Judge Khalil*. The series is about a young black American teenager on his way to becoming a young teenage real-life judge.

In 2013, the animation video went viral and was published on the Ebony Magazine and Historical Black Colleges and Universities (HBCU) Digest sites and received thousands of views. We raised more than $5,000 towards diversifying animation, and educating the youth on non-traditional career paths for people of color and HBCU awareness. I strongly believe in creating positive images for women and people of color through film, theatre and animation.

As a millennial youth leader continue to speak to student crowds at college and community events. Recognition as a youth leader is empowering and inspirational. It is the one reward that keeps you want to grow more and more.

If someone asked me "Why should young people get involved in youth leadership activities?" I will tell them that it teaches youth how to network and build relationships. It gives young people a voice, a chance to be heard and the opportunity to change the world. Above all, networking is key. It's not always what you know. It's who you know.

- Alexis Small, Paramount, CA.
Alexis Small Productions, LLC

THE TIME IS NOW TO BUILD BRIDGES

As youth leadership coordinators, we see and hear a variety of conversational exchanges between young people. Some years ago, in a youth leadership workshop session, two youths were talking in the corner of the room, a 15 year old young man and a 17 year old young lady. The young man appeared to be frustrated, angry and downright fuming mad. He said he was angry that no one was listening to him. The young lady appeared to be agitated and annoyed as well, by his unwillingness to move on from the issue at hand.

She told him, "Why are you so mad at them? You need to let it go." The young man paced back and forth, really upset, saying, "I can't. They really disrespected me and I need to do something about it."

Realizing her efforts were futile at changing his mind, she began to walk away. When the young man tried to get her attention, the young lady swiftly turned to look at him directly, stuck out her hand in front of his face and blurted out, "Look! As my mom says, you need to build a bridge and get over it!"

Sound familiar? Of course telling someone to "build a bridge and get over it" is typically a euphemism or cynical way of telling someone to stop making a mountain out of a molehill. But is it okay for one young person to assume his or her peer is overreacting about an issue? Are issues like these really minor? And, if unaddressed, isn't there a potential for these little issues grow larger, possibly leading an upset youth to behave in a potentially destructive manner? We don't want them to build a bridge to get over an issue, rather instead build a bridge to cross over to a solution.

This is why engaging youth leadership training is needed, to help young people bridge the gap between their feelings of anger and frustration and the realization of knowing there is a solution to their issues; not to get over an issue, but to overcome it.

Bridges are typically seen as helping people get from one location to another, or in this case, transcend from one feeling to another. Humorously speaking, one may be thinking of the London Bridge, a dental bridge, or a famous celebrity like Jeff Bridges. No, not these bridges. We are talking about bridges that can help lead young people to solutions dealing with anger and peer pressure . . . bridges that can close the gap of violence and hate crimes among our youth. Our young people need bridges.

Let's put some time perspective to these issues. According to a 2000 American Medical Association (AMA) study conducted on in youth deaths back in 1933, 75% of deaths were of natural causes. Sixty years later in 1993, that changed to 80% of youth deaths due to youth homicidal crime. In 2006, a study by the Josephson Institute revealed 42% of high school boys surveyed expressed that was okay to hit or threaten someone who made them angry. And the study reported that up to 40% of boys had committed an act of violence by the age of 17.

These days, youth violence is the third leading cause of death for young people between the ages of 15 and 24. While the media covers horrific mass shootings like Sandy Hook, rarely reported is that in America, an average of 13 young people die each day from violence (Youth Violence, 2019).

In the United Kingdom, serious youth violence is a social emergency. In a 2019 article in *The Guardian*, Home Affairs Committee Chair Yvette Cooper, stated, "teenagers are dying on our streets . . . Serious violence has gotten worse after a perfect storm of youth service cuts, police cuts, more children being excluded from school and a failure of statutory agencies to keep them safe" (Grierson, 2019).

There is a way to reduce the tension. Strong adult social support can help prevent violence among teen boys growing up in poor neighborhoods, new research showed, according to a study published online in September 2019 in *JAMA Network Open* (Preidti, 2019).

Today, a significant opportunity exists to help our youth avoid violence and violent situations. An increase in youth leadership training can help bridge that gap. We need to give back, to help our youths overcome peer pressure and violence. Building bridges of youth leadership training can be the key. Programs like the Toastmasters Youth Leadership Program and Training Dynamics Network can help youth embrace leadership skills to create better awareness and combat fatal dispositions of violence.

Youth leadership training helps youth make better choices, better decisions and defuse violence through effective communication skills. Parents, schools and communities need to increase their involvement in investing in the development of more youth leadership programs. It's time to learn more, train more, contribute more and give more.

The next time someone tells a young person to "build a bridge and get over it," think of the despair and hopelessness facing our young people. Let's not just tell our young people to build a bridge to get over it . . . let's help them build a bridge to overcome it.

- David A. Kitchen

APPENDIX

Youth Leadership Program (YLP) Pre-Registration Timelines		
ACTION ITEMS	TIME FRAME	NOTES
Finalized Preparation Package: Includes Welcome/Introduction Letter & Enrollment Registration Packets (5 pages). Also prepare a "student/participant" list for Client to use.	8 Weeks Prior	
Identify Client: Establish students/school, Point of Contact(s), Location	6 Weeks Prior	
Meet with Point-of-Contacts. Establish commitment and time deadlines. Discuss Enrollment Packet and discuss the Interview Dates for each student. Discuss number of student and how they will be selected. Also determine Room, Hours, Tables & Chairs needed, bathrooms, food facilities, etc.	5 Weeks Prior	
Provide Client with appropriate amount of packets, the student sheet and instructions on follow up.	4 Weeks Prior	
Mail/Distribute Welcome Letter and Enroll Registration Packets to the selected students	4 Weeks Prior	
Follow up with Point of Contact(s) to monitor progress/time deadlines. Monitor progress and keep YLP team informed.	4 - 2 Weeks Prior	
Procure Food and Snack Plans for students and staff	3 Weeks Prior	
Collect Forms/Packet from the Client. Complete the Student List.	3 Weeks Prior	
Confirm that the Interview Dates are accepted by the students, and times that the students will be available for the interviews.	3 Weeks Prior	
Communicate the Interview Dates and Hours to the YLP Committee members who will be interviewing.	3 Weeks Prior	
Conduct the interviews with the students. Use Student sheet to indicate which students have been interviewed.	1 - 2 Weeks Prior	
Establish time to set up the facility/room and registration process.	7 Days Prior	
Confirm all Equipment is ready and Food providers are ready	7 Days Prior	
Set up facility, room, training area(s), flip charts, etc.	1 Day Prior	
Welcome Students and Start Program	**May 31, 2019**	

Figure 1. Timeline for Youth Leadership Program (2019) – Courtesy TDN

APPENDIX

Youth Leadership Program Training Budget

Organization: _____ Year: _____
Department: _____ Submitted by: _____
Annual training allotment: _____
1Q Budget: $0   3Q Budget: $0   Total Budget: $0
2Q Budget: $0   4Q Budget: $0

1st Quarter Training Budget

Line	Item	Description/Justification	Qty.	Unit Cost/Rate	Total
1	Program Development				$0
2	Courseware Purchase				0
3	Certification Cost				0
4	Recognition Awards				0
5	Program Advertising				0
6	Facility Rental				0
7	Program Materials				0
8	Technical Equipment				0
9	Consulting Fees				0
10	Facilitator/Trainer				0
11	Trainer Assistant				0
12	Travel				0
13	Per Diem				0
14	Printing				0
15					0
				Grand Total	$0

Figure 2.- Sample Budget for Youth Leadership – Courtesy TDN (2016)

Sample Program Evaluation
(for program participants)

1. I think the youth leadership development program overall is:

Poor		OK		Excellent
1	2	3	4	5

2. On a scale of 1(lowest) to 5 (highest), rate the program leaders:

___They understood what they taught
___They communicated clearly
___I felt I could go to them with questions and problems
___My mentor did a good job
___Their goals and expectations were clear
___They gave me chances to lead

Anything else you'd like to say about the leaders?
_____
_____

3. What program activities did you like the most this year? Why?
_____
_____

4. What program activities did you like the least this year? Why?
_____
_____

5. I increased my skills or knowledge the most in *(check all that apply)*:

☐ Character Traits of Leaders
☐ Understanding Types of Leadership
☐ Team Building
☐ Listening Skills
☐ Problem Solving Skills
☐ Relating to Peers

Figure 3. –Sample of Evaluation Form for Youth Leadership – Amy Sherman (2004)

APPENDIX

Student Feedback Survey

1. How satisfied are you with your current learning in my class?
   Circle one number: 0 = completely dissatisfied; 10 = completely satisfied

   1 2 3 4 5 6 7 8 9 10

2. Thinking about my classroom teaching, fill in the blank: It would be helpful for me if my teacher spent:

   MORE TIME:
   _____

   LESS TIME:
   _____

3. With respect to homework and other assignments for completion outside class time, circle one:

5. What things about my teaching, our procedures, our classroom, our assignments, etc. are satisfactory and what needs improvement? Please be as specific as you can!

   TEACHING:

   PROCEDURES:

   CLASSROOM:

   ASSIGNMENTS:

Figure 4 - Sample Student Feedback Survey – Edutopia (2016)

LIST OF YOUTH ORGANIZATIONS

The following is a list of some of the youth organizations that focus on providing youth leadership activities and socialization for young people.

4-H Organization [Youth Development]
www.4-h.org

Bureau of Exchanges and Cultural Affairs (All youth programs)
www.exchanges.state.gov/non-us/program/youth-leadership-programs

Boys and Girls Club of America [Youth Development]
www.bgca.org

Boys Scouts of America (BSA) [Youth Leadership]
www.scouting.org

Detroit Food Academy (DFA) [Youth Leadership]
www.detroitfoodacademy.org

Girls Club of Los Angeles (GCLA) [Youth Development]
www.girlsclubla.org

Girl Scouts of America (GSA) [Youth Development]
www.girlscouts.org

Making Choices Mentoring Program (MCMP) [Youth Development]
www.teensmakingchoices.org

Neighbors Empowering Youth (NEY) [Youth Technology]
www.neypcworkshop.org

Special Olympics Southern California (SOSC) [Youth Leadership]
www.sosc.org/youthleadership

Training Dynamics Network (TDN) [Youth Leadership]
www.trainingdynamics.org

Toastmasters International [Communication and Leadership]
www.toastmasters.org

Youth Empowerment Solutions (YES) [Youth Empowerment]
www.yes.sph.umich.edu

REFERENCE LIST

Bhagi, U. E-Learning Industry (2017) 12 Reasons Why Project-Based Leaning is Better. Retrieved from URL: https://elearningindustry.com/project-based-learning-better-traditional-classroom

Change Conversations, (2018), Retrieved from URL: https://www.marketing-partners.com/conversations2/how-to-attract-young-people-to-your-nonprofit

Community Tool Box, (2019), Chapter 41, Retrieved from URL: https://ctb.ku.edu/en/table-of-contents/maintain/reward-accomplishments/goal-attainment/main

Clark, H.B., Transition to Independence Process (TIP) System: A Community-Based Model for Improving the Outcomes of Youth and Young Adults with EBD; Stars Behavioral Health Group, Long Beach, CA. (2010).

Davis, C., Final Report – v.3 Page 24 Human Service Collaborative Youth/Young Adult Engagement July 29, (2016)

Davis, C. , Best Practices in Youth Engagement, (2016), Retrieved from URL: (http://www.endowmentforhealth.org/uploads/resources/id115/Youth_engagement_best_practices.pdf)

Detroit Food Academy, (2019), Retrieved from URL: https://detroitfoodacademy.org/who-we-are/directors@detroitfoodacademy.org

DoSomething, (2019), Retrieved from URL: https://www.dosomething.org/facts/11-facts-about-high-school-dropout-rates

DoOneThing, (2019), Retrieved from URL: https://www.doonething.org/quotes/youth-quotes.htm

Dorsey, J. Generations Z and Millennial Researcher (2019), Retrieved from URL: https://jasondorsey.com/bio/

Dorsey, J. Generations Z and Millennial Researcher (2019), Retrieved from URL: https://twitter.com/jasondorsey?lang=ga

Eades, J., INC., (2018), Retrieved from URL: https://www.inc.com/john-eades/6-simple-reasons-all-leaders-should-be-actively-using-social-media.html

Finamore, E. , AllAbout, (2019), Retrieved from URL: https://www.allaboutschoolleavers.co.uk/news/article/318/the-top-10-challenges-facing-young-people-today)

EMpower, (2016), Retrieved from URL: https://empowerweb.org/youth-development-tools/category/evaluating-programs-for-youth

Expedite-Consulting; (2019). Retrieved from URL: http://expedite-consulting.com/10-millennial-leaders-around-the-world

Gladstone, S., Numundo (2013), Retrieved from URL: http://blog.numundo.org/2015/01/09/10-ways-to-empower-youth-leadership-shayna-gladstone/

Global Teen Leaders, Threedotdash, (2019), Retrieved from URL: https://www.threedotdash.org/2019-global-teen-leaders

REFERENCE

Grierson, J. (the Guardian UK, Retrieved from URL: (2019),https://www.theguardian.com/uk-news/2019/jul/31/action-on-rise-in-youth-violence-completely-inadequate-say-mps

Hicks, J., Ph.D, Psychology Today, (2018). Retrieved from URL: https://www.psychologytoday.com/us/blog/raising-parents/201805/why-do-todays-youth-seem-so-different)

Katemba, Dr. C., Academia, (2015), Retrieved from URL: https://www.academia.edu/18262390/Guidelines For Organising Training_Workshops-and_seminars

Kent, P., Stanford Univ. Innovation Review, (2017), retrieved from URL: https://ssir.org/articles/entry/the_recipe_for_youth_success

Kolb, D., Kolb. A., SAGE Handbook of Management Learning, Education and Development (2006), Retrieved from URL: (https://books.google.com/books?hl=en&lr=&id=Om3nZSDGKNUC&oi=fnd&pg=PA42&dq=experiential+learning+approach&ots=vshsYkPbke&sig=ns_C-WRqssNrQSyTctI-07KxoE8

Lovestrand, K. Climate Generation (2011), Retrieved from URL: https://www.climategen.org/blog/key-ingredients-for-successful-youth-engagement/

Martin, J. (2018). Retrieved from URL: http://www.msue.anr.msu.edu/news/icebreakers_build_connections_and_energizer_youth_in_group_settings

Mort, A., Blogsite, (2019), Retrieved from URL: https://www.andymort.com/practice/

Murray, J., Lagacee, (2019), Retrieved from URL: https://www.legacee.com/motivation-at-work/what-is-motivation/

Pew Research Center, Social Media Fact Sheet, (2019), Retrieved from URL: https://www.pewinternet.org/fact-sheet/social-media/

Preidti, R., US News (2019), Retrieved from URL: https://www.usnews.com/news/health-news/articles/2019-09-13/adult-support-can-make-the-difference-for-boys-from-tough-neighborhoods

Ramsey, M., Short Story: Falling Off Bike (2012). Retrieved from URL: http://marshallramsey.com/?p=9191

Reich, J. , Unitarian Universalist Assoc., "A Few Good Ideas," (2005), Retrieved from URL: https://www.uua.org/sites/live-new.uua.org/files/ygactivities.pdf

Saggers, S., Palmer, D., Royce, P., Wilson, L. and Charlton, A. (2004) Alive and Motivated: Department of Family and Community Services on behalf of NYARS, Canberra. Retrieved from URL: https://researchrepository.murdoch.edu.au/id/eprint/42360/

Self Help For The Elderly, (2019), Retrieved from URL: https://www.selfhelpelderly.org/our-services/additional-projects/youth-leadership-technology-program

Shaw, A. , TheMuse, (2019), Retrieved from URL: https://www.themuse.com/advice/7-ways-organized-chaos-can-lead-to-great-things-at-work

Spataro, J., DDI, Leader Pulse (2019). Retrieved from URL: https://www.ddiworld.com/blog/august-2019/what-generation-z-wants-from-leaders)

Social Solutions, (2019), Retrieved from URL: https://www.socialsolutions.com/blog/at-risk-youth-statistics/

Stars Training Academy, (2010),Retrieved from URL: https://www.starsinc.com/programs/stars-training/

Teacher Learning and Professional Development Vol. 1, No. 1, (2016), pp. 61 – 72 21st- century learning, educational reform, and tradition:

Conceptualizing professional development in a progressive age Theodore M. Christou* Queen's University, Canada

TeachThought,(2017), Retrieved from URL: https://www.teachthought.com/pedagogy/21-simple-ideas-to-improve-student-motivatio/

Total Dreamer, (2017), Retrieved from URL: https://www.totaldreamer.com/practice-short-inspirational-story/

Warfield, Z., Yes Magazine (2019), Retrieved from URL: https://www.yesmagazine.org/peace-justice/food-program-kitchen-classroom-detroit-students-learn-leaderhip-20190507

Weiss, C. H. (1998). Evaluation (2nd Ed). Upper Saddle River, NJ: Prentice Hall; Bronte-Tinkew, J., Joyner, K., & Allen, T. (2007). Five steps for selecting an evaluator: A guide for out-of-school time practitioners (Research-to-Results Brief, 2007-32). Washington, DC: Child Trends.

Youth.gov (2007), Retrieved from URL: 1https://youth.gov/evidence-innovation/monitoring-evaluating#_ftn

Young Violence in America Assoc., (2019) , Retrieved from URL: https://yipa.org/youth-violence-america/

FIGURES LIST

Figure 1 – Training Dynamics Network (TDN), (2019), Youth Leadership Program Timeline

Figure 2 – Training Dynamics Network, (TDN), (2016) Youth Leadership Program Training Budget

Figure 3 – Sherman, A., (2004), Sample Program Evaluation

Figure 4 – Edutopia, (2016), Student Feedback Survey. Retrieved from URL: http://www.edutopia.org/practice/student-surveys-using-student-voice-improve-teaching-and-learning

ACKNOWLEDGMENTS

First and foremost, to God, who makes all things possible and for paving the way through this incredible journey.

To my wife Shirley Kitchen and our boys, Davidlee and Christopher for being my inspiration.

To my brother Michael Lattimore for your technical guidance and mentoring.

To my editor Cynthia Gellis for the amazing work as development and chief editor.

To the wonderful leaders who contributed to this book and all of the youth who have gone through the TDN youth leadership program, along with the schools, institutions and professionals who trusted me to work with their young people.

To my colleagues of the Toastmasters International and the Youth Leadership Programs, for fostering the inspiration for this book.

ABOUT THE CONTRIBUTORS

The following pages are dedicated to acknowledging leaders who contributed their experiences, stories and words of wisdom. Thank you for your insight and testimonials to the power of engaging our youth leaders.

Monique Debi: Baltimore, Maryland - Principal of the Fort Worthington Elementary/Middle School, considered now as a "21st Century School." Ms. Debi earned the distinguished honor of Lead Teacher in Baltimore City Schools' first cohort of lead teachers in 2014, and has been recognized for her innovative approaches to project-based learning. Ms. Debi holds a Bachelor of Arts in History from Morgan State University, a Master in the Art of Teaching (MAT) in Elementary Education from Johns Hopkins University and is currently a doctoral candidate at Walden University. Visit the school's website at www.baltimorecityschools.org.

Keith Jackson: Chino Hills, California - Founder and CEO of the ETEC Consulting Group and a leadership trainer. Keith leads a team of engineering experts in operational risk management (RMP) and process safety (PSM) compliance solutions for the petroleum, chemicals, aerospace, biotech, foods, water distribution, and cosmetics industries worldwide. Keith is also a project manager, public speaker and a corporate mentor leader for adult and youth leadership programs. Keith holds a Bachelor of Science and a Master of Science in Engineering from University of Illinois, as well as a Master of Science in Business Administration from the University of Chicago. Visit his website at www.etecconsulting.com.

Me'Lisa James: Sacramento, California – a native of the Davis, California area and mentoring sessions (POMS) director at Project Optimism, Inc. Me'Lisa is high school teacher turned education programs manager, with a diverse professional background in both formal and informal educational settings in the California K-12 public education system. Me'Lisa holds a teaching credential in Social Science, and a Bachelor of Arts in History and Master of Arts & Education in Lesson Studies and Program Development, both from the University of California, Davis. Visit Project Optimism and the Sankofa Project at www.projectoptimism.org.

Michelle King: Long Beach, California - pre-ops coordinator for Orange Coast Memorial Hospital, an evangelist with the Power of Praise Ministries and a trainer and public speaker. . As an evangelist and a leadership council member, she heads up the youth leader department, working with youth on honing their communication and leadership skills. Michelle is a Distinguished Toastmaster with Toastmasters International and holds a certification as a CyberSAFE end-user. Visit her at www.trainingdynamics.org.

Davidlee Kitchen: Cypress, California - Co-Founder and Chief Operating Officer of the TV award-winning Billionaire Burger Boyz (BBB), LLC. BBB is a two-time winner of the Food Network TV Show *Guy's Grocery Games*, was featured on the Cooking Channel's *Food Truck Nation* and featured in numerous media platforms. Davidlee was honored by L.A. Council President Herb Wesson with a proclamation from the City of Los Angeles for his community leadership, spearheading the monthly Leimert Park Friday Nite Block Party in Los Angeles, California. Visit the company's website at www.billionaireburgerboyz.com.

Michael Lattimore: Altadena, California - Cybersecurity Awareness Evangelist, retired after 25 years with Southern California Edison (SCE). He is a founding board member of Internet Association of Security Awareness Professionals (IASAP), executive board member of the Freedom to Choose Project, chief cyber operations officer at Training Dynamics Network, and co-author of *Volunteer Leadership: 7 Disciplines to Undisputed Success*. Michael delivers presentations and workshops specializing in creating and promoting security awareness

ABOUT THE CONTRIBUTORS

culture in corporate and community environments. Michael holds a Bachelor of Arts in Religious Studies from the University of Transformational Studies & Leadership, and a Master of Arts in Psychology from the University of Santa Monica. Visit his website at www.mikelattimore.org

Justin Maclin: Sacramento, California - director of development at the University of California, Davis, CEO of Maclin Motivation, LLC and author of *The Philosophy of HUSTLE*. Justin is a volunteer and mentor with Project Optimism. His book is a self-help memoir of his life and his philosophy of empowering people to pursue and live their life goals with purpose. Justin holds a Bachelor of Science in Sports Administration and a Master in Higher Education Administration, both from Louisiana State University. Visit his company website at www.maclinmotivationhptp.com.

Sam Paano: Lakewood, California - A food and engineer techy. He is executive chef and founder of Gourmet Conspiracy, and a security systems designer at P2S, Inc. As a chef and caterer since January 2000, he and his wife Deady provide affordable gourmet services to the community by growing their own organic and sustainable produce, protein, and supplies. Sam is a Distinguished Toastmaster with Toastmasters International and a culinary graduate of the Kitchen Academy in Hollywood, California.

Jen Rusciano: Detroit, Michigan - co-founder and executive director of the Detroit Food Academy. In 2010, she received a Thomas J. Watson Fellowship award to explore the social, economic, and environmental impact of chocolate production on small scale cacao farming communities around the world. As executive director, Jen supports the organization in various capacities, from vision creation, strategic planning and budgeting to administrative functions, food systems education, culture-building and program facilitation. Jen holds a Bachelor of Arts in Geography from Colgate University.
Visit her website at www.detroitfoodacademy.org.

Alexis Small: Paramount, California – social media expert, owner and CEO of Alexis Small Productions, LLC. Alexis is the creator, writer and producer of the web series *23 & Graduated*, which aired on ABC, NBC, CBS, FOX and MYNET targeting the millennium market. She is also the creator and producer of an animated series *Judge Khalil*, a coming-of-age story about an African American boy with big dreams of becoming an actual real-life judge at the age of 12 years old. Alexis holds a Bachelor of Arts in Journalism and Media Studies from Bennett College in Greensboro, North Carolina. Visit her series and website at www.alexissmallproductions.com.

Everette Williams: Los Angeles, California - Retired teacher, after 49 years with the Los Angeles Unified School District. For more than 16 years he has been lending his teaching and leadership skills to help build youth leaders in District One Toastmasters International. As a Distinguished Toastmaster, Everette has been recognized by the Los Angeles County of Parks and Recreation for his outstanding leadership as District One youth leadership chairperson, and has been honored with the District One Toastmasters Roy D. Graham Lifetime Achievement and the Lydia Boyd Communications and Leadership Awards. Everette holds a Bachelor of Arts in Education and a Master of Arts in Instructional Media and Technology.

ABOUT THE AUTHOR

DAVID A. KITCHEN is the founder and CEO of Training Dynamics Network, a community-based youth/adult leadership organization, and the author of *Volunteer Leadership: 7 Disciplines to Undisputed Success*. A professional speaker, trainer, leadership coach and publisher, David has 30+ years of executive and volunteer management experience. His youth leadership program has received congressional recognition for outstanding leadership in the community. His management and leadership experience includes United Airlines, Los Angeles Times, 20th Century Fox, DirectTV, American Honda Motor Co. , Devry University and Platt College.

David's leadership programs have been acclaimed by fortune 500 companies, unified school districts, non-profit organizations and workforce agencies. His youth leadership experience includes serving in Toastmasters International, Boy Scouts of America., Catholic Youth Organization, Paramount Junior Athletes Association and the Boy Scouts of America. In Toastmasters International, David is a five-time Distinguished Toastmaster (DTM) and member of District One Speakers Bureau. Since 2001 he has served as a district governor, parliamentarian and youth leadership chair, and has received numerous awards in excellence in education & training, marketing and youth leadership.

David is a CyberSAFE end-user trainer, holds Associate of Arts degrees in Journalism and Communications, a Bachelor of Science in Business Administration and Management from the University of Phoenix and a Master of Business Administration from Western Governors University. Visit his website at www.trainingdynamics.org.

OTHER BOOKS

Volunteer Leadership: 7 Disciplines to Undisputed Success

Rough Writers Anthology 2019: Moments in Space & Time

Stories by the Rough Writers 2018: From Speeches to Books

TDN delivers comprehensive training that employs "real-world" solutions. Seminars are tailored to meet the needs of individuals and organizations large or small. Explore inspirational and technical topics proven to effect positive change and organizational success. All training is experiential using relevant techniques that sustain and reinforce positive results.

TEAM LEADERSHIP

Team Collaboration
Communications
Strategic Planning

YOUTH LEADERSHIP

Intro to Youth Leadership
Advanced Youth Leadership
Cyber Youth Leadership
Entrepreneurial Leadership

CYBER LEADERSHIP

Social Media Awareness
Data Privacy Management
Cyber Leadership

Reserve Your Workshop Today

Visit our Website: www.trainingdynamics.org
Phone : (562) 548-2284 or Email: info@trainingdynamics.org

cyberSAFE™

WHY CyberSAFE?

A single email can lead to a multi-million dollar breach in seconds. People responsible are not even aware of their mistake nor of the dangers

CyberSAFE™ will enable youth, adults, teachers & employees to identify the most common risks in using conventional, mobile, and cloud technologies to protect against cyber threats.

Cost of a Data Breach

$3.86 million
Average cost of a data breach

$148
Average cost per record
IBM 2018

COMPLIANCE

Cyber awareness training is no longer a nice-to-have option for organizations. Thousands of laws across the globe and monetary penalties are on the rise.

Studies show implementing a company-wide cyber awareness training program can **reduce incidents by up to 70%** and be able to reduce **cybersecurity insurance premiums**.

92%
Verizon's 2018 Breach Investigations Report, email is responsible for 92 percent of malware.

READINESS ASSESSMENT

Measure your level of preparedness against cyber threats with FREE **CyberSAFE Readiness Assessment**. Receive a free readiness report by redeeming your free access code CMKXFWEF3V at certnexus.com/readiness.

AWARENESS

Empower decisions makers, leaders and youth to lead and put emerging technology into practice.

Training Dynamics Network
(562) 548-2284
cybersafe@trainingdynamics.org
www.trainingdynamics.org/cybersafe

Certnexus.com

www.ingramcontent.com/pod-product-compliance
Lightning Source LLC
Chambersburg PA
CBHW070851050426
42453CB00012B/2134